The Ways of Providence

THE WAYS OF PROVIDENCE

Religion & George Washington

Frank E. Grizzard, Jr.

BUENA VISTA · CHARLOTTESVILLE, VIRGINIA

Copyright © 2005 by Frank E. Grizzard, Jr.

All rights reserved, including the right of reproduction in whole or in part in any form.

Manufactured in the United States of America

1 3 5 7 9 10 8 6 4 2

Library of Congress Control Number: 2005926784
The Ways of Providence: Religion and George Washington
Frank E. Grizzard, Jr.
Includes Bibliographical References and Index.
p. cm.
1. Washington, George, 1732–1799—Religion.
2. Religion—United States History—18th century. 3. Presidents—United States—Biography. 4. Burk, William Jackson, 1867–1933—Writings.
I. Grizzard, Frank E., Jr. II. Title.
ISBN 0-9768238-1-0 (softcover : alk. paper)

MARINER PUBLISHING
a Division of Mariner Companies, Inc.
212 East 21st Street
Buena Vista, Virginia 24416-2716
http://www.marinermedia.com

This book is printed on acid-free paper meeting requirements of the American Standard for Permanence of Paper for Printed Library Materials.

Printed in the United States of America

For My Children

Pamela Jewel

Sarah Faith

Philip Noah

Hannah Elizabeth Grace

Mary Katherine

Margaret Augusta

Tell your children of it,
and let your children tell their children,
and their children another generation. —Joel 1:3

Contents

The Ways of Providence   1

Pohick Church, Truro Parish   15

Valley Forge   19

Documents   25

George Washington's Prayer Book   51

Index   117

Washington Praying at Valley Forge, c.1866
Painted by H. Brueckner
Engraved by John C. McRae

The Ways of Providence

As a practicing Christian, or more specifically, Episcopalian, Washington's behavior is known with some exactitude. He was a lifelong member of the Anglican Church in Virginia, in which he was baptized, married, and served as godfather for the children of various relatives and friends. From 1763 to 1784 he was a member of the Truro Parish Vestry, serving as a churchwarden on three occasions, and taking an active part in its affairs until 1774. Yet despite his support of the church, Washington attended religious services sparingly. According to his diaries, he went to church about once a month while at Mount Vernon, choosing instead to read, ride, hunt, and entertain on Sundays. During his presidency, perhaps more conscious of his example, he went more frequently, attending St. Paul's Chapel and Trinity Church in New York City and Christ Church and St. Peter's in Philadelphia. Even then he did not partake of the sacrament of the Lord's Supper, although his wife was a "habitual communicant." One minister, Dr. James Abercrombie, recalled in 1831 the Washington family's attendance at Christ Church, observing that "on Sacrament Sundays, Gen'l Washington immediately after the Desk and Pulpit services, went out with the greater part of the congregation, always leaving Mrs. Washington with the communicants, she *invariably* being one, I considered it my duty, in a sermon on Public Worship, to state the unhappy tendency of *example,* particularly those in elevated stations, who invariably turned their backs upon the celebration of the Lord's Supper. I acknowledge the remark was intended for the President, as such, he received it." Indeed, Washington understood that the minister referred to him and discussed the matter with an unnamed U.S. senator during the following week. The senator, Abercrombie continued, "told me he had dined the day before with the President, who in the course of the conversation at the table, said, that on the preceding Sunday, he had received a very just reproof from the pulpit, for always leaving the church before the administration of the Sacrament; that he honored the preacher for his integrity and candour; that he had never considered the influence of his example; that he would never again give cause for the repetition of the reproof; and that, as he had never been a communicant, were he to become one of them, it would be imputed to an ostentatious display of religious zeal arising altogether from his elevated station. Accordingly, he afterwards never came on the morning of Sacrament Sunday, tho' at other times, a constant attendant in the morning."

Religion and George Washington

The most astute observer to date of Washington's religious preferences, Paul F. Boller, in his *George Washington and Religion* (Dallas, Texas, 1962), suggested that Washington's reluctance to take communion arose from the feeling that his mind and heart were not in "a proper condition to receive the sacrament," and that he was unwilling to indulge in hypocrisy.

As for other rituals, Washington on occasion observed the custom of having a blessing pronounced at mealtime, especially if there was a clergyman present to say grace. He apparently did not take the same delight in reading religious pamphlets or sermons as his wife, who did so daily with her granddaughter, Nelly Custis. Perhaps Washington's attitude about his personal practice of religion may be seen in his behavior (as recorded in his diaries) while on the presidential tour of New England in November 1789: "It being contrary to Law & disagreeable to the People of this State (Connecticut) to travel on the Sabbath day and my horses after passing through such intolerable Roads wanting rest, I stayed at [Isaac] Perkins's Tavern (which by the bye is not a good one) all day — and a meeting House being with in a few rod of the Door, I attended Morning & evening Service, and heard very lame discourses from a Mr. [Enoch] Pond."

It is difficult to trace any changes in Washington's religious beliefs over time. He seems from an early age to have developed the attitudes toward religion and habits of church attendance that he would carry throughout his life. By the time of his earliest surviving writings he apparently had imbibed generously of Stoic philosophy, either directly through his own study, or indirectly, perhaps by his association with the Fairfax family at Belvoir, said to be given over to Stoicism, which thereafter filtered his religious and philosophical opinions. As a philosophy of life Stoicism is simple, practical, reasonable, and humanitarian. As such it had elements in common with the fraternal organizations familiar to Washington such as Freemasonry. The Stoic philosophy embraced the classical virtues and reinforced the Deist beliefs current in the eighteenth century. Boller notes that Washington relied upon "a Grand Designer along Deist lines." His conception of the subject apparently was not as complex or as subtle as that of Benjamin Franklin, Thomas Jefferson, or James Madison, but it was, said Boller, "as deep-seated and meaningful for his life." He formed his religious vocabulary after his usual fashion of borrowing, using, and discarding phrases of language from others as the occasion arose. More often than not Washington referred to God as "Providence" or "Heaven," although he sometimes appealed to the "Director of Human Events," the "Great Ruler of Events," the "Supreme Ruler," the "Governor of the Universe," the "Author of the Universe," the "Supreme Architect of the Universe," the "Grand Architect," the "Author of all good," the "supreme arbiter of events," the "beneficent Being," the "Sovereign Dispenser of life and health," the "Higher Cause," and the "Great Creator."

The qualities attributed to Providence by Washington reveal that he conceived of Providence as an "Omnipotent," "benign," and "beneficient" Being that by "invisible workings" in "Infinite Wisdom" dispensed justice in the affairs of mankind. Astonishment and gratitude were owed this Being. The "ways of Providence" were, he confessed on many occasions, ultimately "inscrutable." Such beliefs are exemplified in Washington's calm, almost detached, acquiescence to the *irreversible* acts of Providence, such as terminal illness or the death of a loved one. An early letter consoling Burwell Bassett for the death of his daughter, for instance, was not dissimilar to condolences that he would write ever after: "The ways of Providence being inscrutable, and the justice of it not to be scanned by the shallow eye of humanity, not to be counter-acted by the utmost efforts of human power or wisdom, resignation, and as far as the strength of our reason and religion can carry us, a cheerful acquiescence to the Divine Will, is what we are to aim." Although he tempered his submission with hope as long as there was the chance that Providence might decree otherwise, once the will of Providence had been manifested there would be no protest from Washington. Where it was yet unknown what course would be taken, however, Washington insisted that individuals had both a need and an obligation to discover and work with Providence. Even his occasional use of the terms "Fate," "Fortune," and "Destiny" were linked with the role of individuals in their own affairs, playing down the fixed nature implied by those words.

What Washington once styled as his "Doctrine of Providence" played a central role in the outcome of not only individuals, but also of peoples and nations. Washington's encounters with enemy gunfire in July 1755 during the disastrous Braddock campaign of the French and Indian War left him convinced that he had been left in the land "of the livg by the miraculous care of Providence, that protected me beyond all human expectation." He had survived despite having two horses shot from under him and four bullets pass through his coat. Providence was involved in defeat, too, for British general Edward Braddock was killed and his troops beaten by a handful of men who only intended to molest and disturb their march. "Victory was their [the enemy's] smallest expectation," he wrote, "but see the wondrous works of Providence! the uncertainty of Human things!" That same uncertainty seemed to characterize the changing fortunes of

> ... *the miraculous care of Providence, that protected me beyond all human expectation* ...

Religion and George Washington

the Revolutionary War, although Washington held firmly to the justness of the American cause and to a belief that Providence ultimately would favor that cause. His General Orders frequently contained appeals to the Almighty for assistance, expressions of thanksgiving for the "remarkable interpositions of Providence," and reminders for the troops to attend divine services.

As time progressed, Washington's faith in the intervention of Providence on behalf of American arms seemed to grow. "It is not a little pleasing, nor less wonderful to contemplate,"

The hand of Providence has been so conspicuous in all this, that he must be worse than an infidel that lacks faith. . . .

he wrote while at White Plains, New York, in August 1778, "that after two years Manæuvring and undergoing the strangest vicissitudes that perhaps ever attended any one contest since the creation both Armies are brought back to the very point they set out from and, that that, which was the offending party in the beginning is now reduced to the use of the spade and pick axe for defence. The hand of Providence has been so conspicuous in all this, that he must be worse than an infidel that lacks faith, and more than wicked, that has not gratitude enough to acknowledge his obligations, but, it will be time enough for me to turn preacher, when my present appointment ceases; and therefore, I shall add no more on the Doctrine of Providence." After Lord Cornwallis surrendered his army at Yorktown in the fall of 1781, Washington ordered divine services to be attended universally "with that seriousness of Deportment and gratitude of Heart which the recognition of such reiterated and astonishing interpositions of Providence demand of us." In his Farewell Orders to the army on 2 November 1783, Washington again declared that the "singular interposition of Providence in our feeble condition were such, as could scarcely escape the attention of the most unobserving."

It will be time enough for me to turn preacher, when my present appointment ceases. . . .

Although Washington often wrote about the intervention of Providence in human affairs, he only rarely mentioned his beliefs about an afterlife. When a friend named a son after him, Washington wrote to express the hope that "he will live long to enjoy it, long after I have taken my departure for the world of Spirits." On the eve of his leaving Mount Vernon for Philadelphia for the Constitutional Convention, he confided in Robert Morris of his internal conflict about whether to become involved again in a public life: "My first remaining wish being, to glide gently down the stream of life in tranquil retirement till I shall arrive at the world of Sperits." When his mother died in August 1789, at the age of 83, he wrote to console his sister, Betty, expressing the "hope that she is translated to a happier place." To another he referred to being "translated to a happier clime." How literally Washington meant these references to a "happier clime" and a "land of Spirits" is unclear. Certainly there is a detached and almost fatalistic tone about them. In short, he did believe in immortality, but it is unclear whether he held the classical version of one's life and deeds living on in the effects and memory of subsequent generations or the more literal land of spirits, so totally "other worldly" as to be unknowable and hence not worth troubling oneself over. The mention of a happier clime and meeting in the future indicates that he leaned more in favor of some sort of literal afterlife.

> *My first remaining wish being, to glide gently down the stream of life in tranquil retirement till I shall arrive at the world of Spirits. . . .*

For Washington, toleration and liberty of conscience coincided with the civil and social roles of religion. In roles of authority and leadership, both military and civil, Washington invariably appealed to the twin pillars of "human happiness" — religion and morality — to buttress the civil authority and uphold the social underpinnings. He supported chaplains in the army during both the French and Indian and the Revolutionary Wars. Appeals to Providence and days of thanksgiving were frequent during the Revolutionary War and afterward. The latter were ordered by both the Continental and U.S. congresses, but there were also special thanksgiving services ordered by Washington on his own, without any prompting from Congress. Nor was he opposed to public support of religion. When writing George Mason in October 1785 about James Madison's anonymous Memorial and Remonstrance against the religious assessment bill in the Virginia general assembly, Washington expressed his view that, "Altho' no mans sentiments are more opposed to *any kind* of restraint upon religious principles than mine are; yet I must confess, that I am not amongst the number of those who are so much alarmed at the thoughts of making people pay towards the support of that which they profess, if of the denominations of Christians; or declare themselves Jews, Mahomitans or otherwise, & thereby obtain proper relief." Organized religion was, Washington believed, indispensable to the maintenance of morality, which in turn was one of the supports of the social order.

... Of all the dispositions and habits which lead to political prosperity ...

Washington's most public statement on the relationship between religion and society, as he saw it, was included in his Farewell Address to the people of the United

States, made shortly before he retired from his second term as president. "Of all the dispositions and habits which lead to political prosperity," Washington wrote, "Religion and morality are indispensable supports. In vain would that man claim the tribute of Patriotism, who should labour to subvert these great Pillars of human happiness, these firmest props of the duties of Men & citizens. The mere Politician, equally with the pious man ought to respect & to cherish them. A volume could not trace all their connections with private & public felicity. Let it simply be asked where is the security for property, for reputation, for life, if the sense of religious obligation desert the Oaths, which are the instruments of investigation in Courts of Justice? And let us with caution indulge the supposition, that morality can be maintained without religion. Whatever may be conceded to the influence of refined education on minds of peculiar structure — reason & experience both forbid us to expect that National morality can prevail in exclusion of religious principle."

> ... *Religion and morality are indispensable supports.* ...

It is worth noting that in his Farewell Address Washington declined to ascribe any attributes to either the religion or the morality that he referred to. His travels across the country had exposed him to the religious and cultural diversity of the people in the United States, and he apparently gave little thought to the particulars of the beliefs held by any of those people. He long had been a champion of freedom of conviction, or conscience, and he did not hesitate to wish "every temporal and spiritual felicity" to Baptists, Quakers, Catholics, and Jews alike. To the latter he wrote that the new government gave "to bigotry no sanction." To what extent religious opinion entered Washington's changing view of slavery is not known, however.

As president Washington followed the same policy he had when he served as commander in chief of the Continental army — he recognized the importance of organized religion and encouraged participation in it. The theme that America was under the special agency of Providence was stressed in his first inaugural address:

> It would be peculiarly improper to omit in this first official Act, my fervent supplications to that Almighty Being who rules over the Universe, who presides in the Councils of Nations, and whose providential aids can supply every human defect, that his benediction may consecrate to the liberties and happiness of the People of the United States, a Government instituted by themselves for these essential purposes: and may enable every instrument employed in its administration to execute with success, the functions allotted to his charge. In tendering this homage to the Great Author of every public and private good, I assure myself that it expresses your sentiments

not less than my own; nor those of my fellow-citizens at large, less than either. No People can be bound to acknowledge and adore the invisible hand, which conducts the Affairs of men more than the People of the United States. Every step, by which they have advanced to the character of an independent nation, seems to have been distinguished by some token of providential agency. And in the important revolution just accomplished in the system of their United Government, the tranquil deliberations and voluntary consent of so many distinct communities, from which the event has resulted, cannot be compared with the means by which most Governments have been established, without some return of pious gratitude along with an humble anticipation of the future blessings which the past seem to presage.

Throughout his presidency Washington repeated this theme, whether in annual addresses to Congress, official messages to state and local governments, or in letters to civic organizations. Providence also was invoked frequently in Washington's private correspondence.

From time to time Washington also made references not only to religion in general but also to Christianity. His circular letter to the governors of the thirteen states, written at his headquarters in Newburgh, New York, shortly before the end of the war, is perhaps the most explicit:

That God would have you, and the State over which you preside, in his holy protection, that he would incline the hearts of the Citizens to cultivate a spirit of subordination and obedience to Government, to entertain a brotherly affection and love for one another, for their fellow Citizens of the United States at large, and particularly for their brethren who have served in the Field, and finally, that he would most graciously be pleased to dispose us all, to do justice, to love mercy, and to demean ourselves with that Charity, humility, and pacific temper of mind, which were the Characteristicks of the Divine Author of our blessed Religion, and without an humble imitation of whose example in these things, we can never hope to be a happy Nation.

Part of the text of the address, with minor modifications and with the words "Almighty God" placed at the beginning and "Through Jesus Christ Our Lord" at the end, has circulated as "Washington's Prayer."

Religion and George Washington

Pohick Church, Truro Parish

Located a dozen miles south of Alexandria and about five miles from Mount Vernon, in Fairfax County, Virginia, is historic Pohick Church, the church of George Washington. In 1762 Washington was elected a vestryman of Truro Parish, an office concerned less with ecclesiastical affairs than with temporal ones, such as caring for the neighborhood's poorer citizens, overseeing the maintenance of local roads, and policing the movements of indentured servants and slaves from among the area's many plantations. By far the most important parish issue during Washington's thirteen-year tenure was a proposal in 1767 to move the location of the parish meeting-house from the south side of Pohick Creek to a more central location on the main thoroughfare on the other side of the creek. Many, including Washington's neighbor and fellow vestryman George Mason of Gunston Hall, were disinclined to abandon the old site because the bones of their ancestors were resting in the churchyard. Washington, who at the time was one of the parish's two church wardens, allegedly brought to the parochial meeting a plat drawn by himself delineating all the roads and houses in the parish and showing that the proposed location was more accessible than the old to every single one of the church's worshipers. When the issue was decided in favor of the new location, Mason purportedly donned his hat and stalked out of the meeting, ex-claiming, "That's what gentlemen get for engaging in debate with a d—d surveyor!"

Daniel French (1723–1771), a wealthy planter who lived at Rose Hill, his plantation west of Alexandria, contracted with the vestry to build the new church for £877, Virginia currency. (French also owned land in the vicinity of Mount Vernon, including a plantation on Dogue Run adjacent to Mount Vernon that Washington purchased in 1786.) In 1772 the vestry voted to construct an eighteen-by-twenty-four-foot brick vestry house near the church.

Pohick Church, Truro Parish (exterior)

Religion and George Washington

Pohick Church, Truro Parish (interior)

The old Pohick Church building was of simple wooden construction. By contrast the new church, a substantial 3,000-square-foot brick structure, is typical late Georgian parish architecture; its simple rectangular plan includes a low-pitched hip roof with no tower, resembling its northern neighbor, Christ Church, Alexandria, as originally built. Its symmetrical facades contain an unusual feature — rectilinear windows on the first floor and arched windows on the second. The interest and beauty of the building are further enhanced by the use of sandstone to construct the modillioned cornices, angle quoins, and door trim. The church was occupied and badly treated by

Union soldiers during the Civil War, but has since been restored and is used for regular services.

The new church was still under construction when the Washington family had to call upon its rector, Lee Massey, to read the funeral service of the family's youngest member, Patsy Custis, who died of epilepsy on 19 June 1773. The new building was completed the following February, and Washington made known his intentions to frequent the church by having his monogram attached to the door of his pew and by having the pew equipped with drawers in which to set his prayer books and papers. His regular attendance at the church was soon halted by the coming of the Revolutionary War, however, which ended his career as a vestryman as well, although he did not formally resign until February 1784.

Valley Forge

Everyone knows Mason Locke Weems's story of General George Washington praying in the snow at his army's encampment at Valley Forge, Pennsylvania, during the Revolutionary War.

> In the winter of '77, while Washington, with the American army lay encamped at Valley Forge, a certain good old FRIEND, of the respectable family and name of Potts, if I mistake not, had occasion to pass through the woods near head-quarters. Treading his way along the venerable grove, suddenly he heard the sound of a human voice, which as he advanced increased on his ear, and at length became like the voice of one speaking much in earnest. As he approached the spot with a cautious step, whom should he behold, in a dark natural bower of ancient oaks, but the commander in chief of the American armies on his knees at prayer! Motionless with surprise, friend Potts continued on the place till the general, having ended his devotions, arose, and, with a countenance of angel serenity, retired to headquarters: friend Potts then went home, and on entering his parlour called out to his wife,

"Sarah, my dear! Sarah! All's well! all's well! George Washington will yet prevail!"

"What's the matter, Isaac?" replied she; "thee seems moved."

"Well, if I seem moved, 'tis no more than what I am. I have this day seen what I never expected. Thee knows that I always thought the sword and the gospel utterly inconsistent; and that no man could be a soldier and a christian at the same time. But George Washington has this day convinced me of my mistake."

He then related what he had seen, and concluded with this prophetical remark — "If George Washington be not a man of God, I am greatly deceived — and still more shall I be deceived if God do not, through him, work out a great salvation for America."

Originally appearing in the seventeenth-edition of the parson's *Life of Washington* (Philadelphia, 1817), this story, perhaps more than any other, helped popularize the idea in nineteenth-century America that Washington had been a man noted for his deep religious nature and Christian piety. If the picturesque scene of Washington on his knees in the snow pleading with God for the sake of his troops was not enough to make a believer out of those who encountered the story, then the supposed conversion of a peace-loving Quaker into a supporter of the American war effort tended to lend extra credibility. It is true that at the time the Continental troops were at a low point. "It is with infinite pain & concern," wrote Washington after moving his headquarters to Valley Forge in December 1777, "that I transmit Congress the inclosed Copies of Sundry Letters respecting the state of the Commissary's Department. In these matters are not exaggerated. I do not know from what cause this alarming deficiency, or rather total failure of Supplies arises: But unless more vigorous exertions and better regulations take place in that line and immediately, This Army must dissolve." In one of the enclosed letters referring to the hardship at Valley Forge an officer writes, "I have used every Argument my Imagination could invent to make the Soldiers easy, but I despair of being able to do it much longer — When they *have* their Allowance, the Beef has no Fat and the Proportion of Bone so great that it does not suffice Men who have been used to be full fed, the Spirit of stealing and robbing, which God knows was great enough before, must increase if no other bad Consequences follow." Conditions at Valley Forge only got worse as the winter progressed, even though the weather of 1777–1778 was moderate compared with other winters during the Revolutionary War. Thus, it seems, it is no wonder that Washington might have been caught in the act of pleading with the Almighty to provide for his army.

Isaac Potts House
Washington's Valley Forge Headquarters
Photographed by Thomas T. Waterman, 1937
(Library of Congress)

Valley Forge took its name from an iron forge situated on the Schuylkill River, about twenty miles northwest of Philadelphia in Chester and Philadelphia (now Montgomery) counties. Washington chose the location for strategic reasons. It was a natural defensive position which would be difficult for the British now headquartered at Philadelphia to attack without warning. With the Continental army relatively near Philadelphia, British general William Howe would think twice before dispatching troops too far from the city during the winter. And the proximity of Valley Forge to York and Lancaster, where the Continental Congress and the Pennsylvania legislature had fled, would afford Washington an opportunity to assist those bodies if necessary.

Washington reputedly headquartered near the mouth of Valley Creek in Philadelphia County, at a stone mill house that was owned by Quaker Isaac Potts and was occupied at the time by his aunt Deborah Pyewell Potts Hewes, the widow of Thomas Potts II and the wife of Caleb Hewes. The quarters, it as described at the time, were "exceedingly pinched for room." (The headquarters house is shown on an early plan of the Valley Forge encampment drawn by the French engineer Brigadier General Duportail.) Despite the severe hardships associated with the encampment at Valley Forge, the Continental army stayed there until 19 June 1778. Isaac Potts, however, did not live in the area at the time, and the forge was rented to ironmaster William Dewees, despite the fact that Potts's brother, John, was also a successful iron forger. Indeed, a similar account of the prayer story, written by Reverend Nathaniel Randolph Snowden who claimed to have received it directly from Potts himself — but written after Weem's version appeared — names John as the eavesdropper. Discrepancies like this — and others, such as the facts that Isaac Potts did not marry his wife Sarah (mentioned in the story) until 1803, and that clergymen who knew Washington testified that he never knelt during service or at prayer — as well as Weems's proclivity to make up stories out of whole cloth, have cast doubt on the genuineness of the Valley Forge story. (Its authenticity was questioned first beginning in the 1850s.) Nevertheless, whether true or not, the story of Washington on his knees at Valley Forge became and remains a central part of the lore surrounding Washington's religious life.

Documents

... We have abundant reason to rejoice, that in this land the light of truth and reason have triumphed over the power of bigotry and superstition, and that every person may here worship God according to the dictates of his own heart. . . . .

—George Washington
to the New Church in Baltimore, Maryland
c.27 January 1793

The documents presented on these pages are typical of the way George Washington treated the subject of religion in writing, and although they are not comprehensive in scope, they do include some of his most pronounced statements on religion and its role in society.

George Washington became a vestryman for Truro Parish in Fairfax County, Virginia, in 1762, and he was serving as one of the vestry's two churchwardens in 1767 when the vestry decided to replace the old wooden church with a new brick building in a different location. The following document is taken from the Truro Parish Vestry Book, on deposit at the Library of Congress.

Minutes of Truro Parish Vestry
21 September 1769

At a Vestry held for Truro Parish at the Cross Roads leading from Hollis's to Pohick Warehouse Sepr 21st 1769.

A Spott was chosen to fix the new Church upon convenient to the said Cross Roads, & agreeable to a former order of Vestry, bearing date the 20th day of November 1767: A Yard was laid of for the said Church, & a Certain quantity of Land laid of for the use of the said Parish, for which the Said Vestry do agree to pay Daniel French Gent: at the rate of one Guinea per Acre, for what the same shall Measure.

At the same time, the said Daniel French, who on the third Day of March last, undertook to Build the Church for the sum of Eight hundred, Seventy and Seven Pounds Current Money of Virginia, agreeable to a Plan then exhibited, did execute an agreement, and gave Bond for the Performance thereof, agreeable to a Contract enter'd into with the Vestry, on the said third day of March, and order'd to be Ratified and Confirm'd, by certain Instruments of Writing on the Seventh Day of April following; but which, for want of a Meeting of Vestry on that day, and the frequent Disapointments since, has never been done till now.

Resolv'd that the Church-Wardens for the time being, do in behalf of the Parish, procure from the said Daniel French a proper Conveyance of the Lot or Parcell of Land aforementioned.

Resolv'd that the Church-Wardens Receive from Mr Alexander Henderson, the Money that remain in his hands due to the Parish, & pay to Mr Daniel French, the sum of Two hundred Pounds, being the first payment for the new Church.

Resolv'd that the Honble George Wm Fairfax, George Washington & George Mason Esqrs. Captn Daniel McCarty & Mr Edward Payne, do View & examin the Building from time to time, as they or any three of them shall see fitting to whom the undertaker is to give notice when the different Metearials are ready.

Daniel McCarty C:W:	John Posey
Edward Payne	William Gardner
George Washington	Tz. Ellzey
George W: Fairfax	

Truly Recorded,
John Barry Clk Vestry

Washington wrote the following letter to George Mason in reply to one of the previous day from Mason concerning James Madison's anonymous Memorial and Remonstrance against Religious Assessment, presented to the Virginia General Assembly in June 1785, which Mason had printed and requested Washington to sign. Washington, however, makes it clear that in principle he did not oppose the assessment bill, which would support teachers or ministers of the Christian religion, or help fund places of worship, in Virginia, by means of taxes levied from the state's religious societies. This letter is from the letter book copy in the Washington Papers at the Library of Congress.

To George Mason
Mount Vernon, October 3, 1785

Dr Sir I have this moment received yours of yesterday's date enclosing a memorial & remonstrance against the assessment Bill, which I will read with attention; at *present* I am unable to do it, on account of company. The Bill itself I do not recollect ever to have read: with *attention* I am certain I never did — but will compare them together.

Altho' no man's sentiments are more opposed to *any kind* of restraint upon religious principles than mine are; yet I must confess, that I am not amongst the number of those who are so much alarmed at the thoughts of making people pay towards the support of that which they profess, if of the denomination of Christians; or declare themselves Jews, Mahomitans or otherwise, & thereby obtain proper relief. As the matter now stands, I wish an assessment had never been agitated — & as it has gone so far, that the Bill could die an easy death; because I think it will be productive of more quiet to the State, than by enacting it into a Law; which, in my opinion, wou'd be impolitic, admitting there is a decided majority for it, to the disqust of a respectable minority. In the first case the matter will soon subside; in the latter, it will rankle, & perhaps convulse, the State. The Dinner Bell rings, & I must conclude with an expression of my concern for your indisposition. Sincerely and affectionately, I am &. &c.

G: Washington

The letter that follows is typical of the replies that Washington sent to the numerous religious bodies across America that addressed him at the end of the Revolutionary War. The original letter is in the George and Katherine David Collection at Tulane University in New Orleans, Louisiana.

To the Reformed German Congregation
of New York City
New York 27th November 1783

Gentlemen The illustrious and happy event, on which you are pleased to congratulate and welcome me to this City, demands all our gratitude; while the favorable sentiments you have thought proper to express of my conduct, entitles you to my warmest acknowledgements.

Disposed, at every suitable opportunity, to acknowledge publicly our infinite obligations to the Supreme Ruler of the Universe, for rescuing our Country from the brink of destruction I cannot fail at this time to ascribe all the honor of our late successes to the same glorious Being. And if my humble exertions have been made in any degree subservient to the execution of the divine purposes, the contemplation of the benediction of Heaven on our righteous cause, the approbation of my virtuous Countrymen, and the testimony of my own conscience, will be a sufficient reward, and augment my felicity beyond anything which the world can bestow.

The establishment of Civil & Religious Liberty was the motive which induced me to the field, the object is attained and it now remains to be my earnest wish and prayer that the citizens of the United States would make a wise and virtuous use of the blessings placed before them; and that the reformed German Congregation in New York may not only be conspicuous for their religious character but as exemplary in support of our inestimable acquisitions, as their Reverend Minister has been in the attainment of them.

Go: Washington

Washington's election to the office of the presidency occasioned addresses from a variety of religious bodies across the new nation, including Baptists, Presbyterians, Roman Catholics, Society of Friends (Quakers), Unitarian Universalists, and Jews. Washington was scrupulous about writing formal replies to the senders of such addresses (as well as to those who sent similar messages from civic and governmental bodies), often times incorporating the language and ideas of the sender's message in his own reply. The following eight letters (copies of each are in the Library of Congress) are representative of such replies.

>To the United Baptist Churches of Virginia
>New York, May 1789

Gentlemen, I request that you will accept my best acknowledgments for your congratulation on my appointment to the first office in the nation. The kind manner in which you mention my past conduct equally claims the expression of my gratitude.

After we had, by the smiles of Heaven on our exertions, obtained the object for which we contended, I retired at the conclusion of the war, with an idea that my country could have no farther occasion for my services, and with the intention of never entering again into public life: But when the exigence of my country seemed to require me once more to engage in public affairs, an honest conviction of duty superseded my former resolution, and became my apology for deviating from the happy plan which I had adopted.

If I could have entertained the slightest apprehension that the Constitution framed in the Convention, where I had the honor to preside, might possibly endanger the religious rights of any ecclesiastical Society, certainly I would never have placed my signature to it; and if I could now conceive that the general Government might ever be so administered as to render the liberty of conscience insecure, I beg you will be persuaded that no one would be more zealous than myself to establish effectual barriers against the horrors of spiritual tyranny, and every species of religious persecution — For you, doubtless, remember that I have often expressed my sentiment, that every man, conducting himself as a good citizen, and being accountable to God alone for his religious opinions, ought to be protected in worshipping the Deity according to the dictates of his own conscience.

While I recollect with satisfaction that the religious Society of which you are Members, have been, throughout America, uniformly, and almost unanimously, the firm friends to civil liberty, and the persevering Promoters of our glorious revolution; I cannot hesitate to believe that they will be the faithful Supporters of a free, yet efficient general Government. Under this pleasing expectation I rejoice to assure them that they may rely on my best wishes and endeavors to advance their prosperity.

In the meantime be assured, Gentlemen, that I entertain a proper sense of your fervent supplications to God for my temporal and eternal happiness.

G: Washington

To the General Assembly of the Presbyterian Church
New York, May 1789

Gentlemen, I receive with great sensibility the testimonial, given by the General Assembly of the Presbyterian Church in the United States of America, of the live and unfeigned pleasure experienced by them on my appointment to the first office in the nation.

Although it will be my endeavor to avoid being elated by the too favorable opinion which your kindness for me may have induced you to express of the importance of my former conduct, and the effect of my future services: yet, conscious of the disinterestedness of my motive it is not necessary for me to conceal the satisfaction I have felt upon finding, that my compliance with the call of my country, and my dependence on the assistance of Heaven to support me in my arduous undertakings, have, so far as I can learn, met the universal approbation of my countrymen.

While I reiterate the possession of my dependence upon Heaven as the source of all public and private blessings; I will observe that the general prevalence of piety, philanthropy, honesty, industry and œconomy seems, in the ordinary course of human affairs are particularly necessary for advancing and confirming the happiness of our country. While all men within our territories are protected in worshipping the Deity according to the dictates of their consciences; it is rationally to be expected from them in return, that they will be emulous of evincing the sincerity of their profession by the innocence of their lives, and the beneficence of their actions: For no man, who is profligate in his morals, or a bad member of the civil community, can possibly be a true Christian, or a credit to his own religious society.

I desire you to accept my acknowledgements for your laudable endeavors to render men sober, honest, and good Citizens, and the obedient subjects of a lawful government; as well as for your prayers to Almighty God for his blessing on our common country and the humble instrument, which he has been pleased to make use of in the administration of it's government.

G. Washington

To the Society of Quakers
October 1789

Gentlemen, I receive with pleasure your affectionate address, and thank you for the friendly Sentiments & good wishes which you express for the Success of my administration, and for my personal Happiness.

We have Reason to rejoice in the prospect that the present National Government, which by the favor of Divine Providence, was formed by the common Counsels, and peaceably established with the common consent of the People, will prove a blessing to every denomination of them. To render it such, my best endeavours shall not be wanting.

Government being, among other purposes, instituted to protect the Persons and Consciences of men from oppression, it certainly is the duty of Rulers, not only to abstain from it themselves, but according to their Stations, to prevent it in others.

The liberty enjoyed by the People of these States, of worshipping Almighty God agreable to their Consciences, is not only among the choicest of their *Blessings,* but also of their *Rights* — While men perform their social Duties faithfully, they do all that Society or the State can with propriety demand or expect; and remain responsible only to their Maker for the Religion or modes of faith which they may prefer or profess.

Your principles & conduct are well known to me — and it is doing the People called Quakers no more than Justice to say, that (except their declining to share with others the burthen of the common defence) there is no Denomination among us who are more exemplary and useful Citizens.

I assure you very explicitly that in my opinion the Consciencious scruples of all men should be treated with great delicacy & tenderness, and it is my wish and desire that the Laws may always be as extensively accomodated to them, as a due regard to the Protection and essential Interests of the Nation may Justify, and permit.

G: Washington

To Roman Catholics in America United States of America (New York)
March 1790

Gentlemen, While I now receive with much satisfaction your congratulations on my being called, by an unanimous vote, to the first station in my Country; I cannot but duly notice your politeness in offering an apology for the unavoidable delay. As that delay has given you an opportunity of realizing, instead of anticipating, the benefits of the general Government; you will do me the justice to believe, that your testimony of the increase of the public prosperity, enhances the pleasure which I should otherwise have experienced from your affectionate address.

I feel that my conduct, in war and in peace, has met with more general approbation than could reasonably have been expected: and I find myself disposed to consider that fortunate circumstance, in a great degree, resulting from the able support and extraordinary candour of my fellow-citizens of all denominations.

The prospect of national prosperity now before us is truly animating, and ought to excite the exertions of all good men to establish and secure the happiness of their Country, in the permanent duration of its Freedom and Independence. America, under the smiles of a Divine Providence — the protection of a good Government — and the cultivation of manners, morals and piety, cannot fail of attaining an uncommon degree of eminence, in literature, commerce, agriculture, improvements at home and respectability abroad.

As mankind become more liberal they will be more apt to allow, that all those who conduct themselves as worthy members of the Community are equally entitled to the protection of civil Government. I hope ever to see America among the foremost nations in examples of justice and liberality. And I presume that your fellow-citizens will not forget the patriotic part which you took in the accomplishment of their Revolution, and the establishment of their Government: or the important assistance which they received from a nation in which the Roman Catholic faith is professed.

I thank you, Gentlemen, for your kind concern for me. While my life and my health shall continue, in whatever situation I may be, it shall be my constant endeavour to justify the favourable sentiments which you are pleased to express of my conduct. And may the members of your Society in America, animated alone by the pure spirit of Christianity, and still conducting themselves as the faithful subjects of our free Government, enjoy every temporal and spiritual felicity.

G. Washington

To the Hebrew Congregation of Savannah, Georgia
c.May 1790

Gentlemen, I thank you with great sincerity for your congratulations on my appointment to the office, which I have the honor to hold by the unanimous choice of my fellow-citizens: and especially for the expressions which you are pleased to use in testifying the confidence that is reposed in me by your congregation.

As the delay which has naturally intervened between my election and your address has afforded an opportunity for appreciating the merits of the federal-government, and for communicating your sentiments of its administration — I have rather to express my satisfaction than regret at a circumstance, which demonstrates (upon experiment) your attachment to the former as well as approbation of the latter.

I rejoice that a spirit of liberality and philanthropy is much more prevalent than it formerly was among the enlightened nations of the earth; and that your brethren will benefit thereby in proportion as it shall become still more extensive. Happily the people of the United States of America have, in many instances, exhibited examples worthy of imitation — The salutary influence of which will doubtless extend much farther, if gratefully enjoying those blessings of peace which (under favor of Heaven) have been obtained by fortitude in war, they shall conduct themselves with reverence to the Deity, and charity towards their fellow-creatures.

May the same wonder-working Deity, who long since delivering the Hebrews from their Egyptian Oppressors planted them in the promised land — whose providential agency has lately been conspicuous in establishing these United States as an independent nation — still continue to water them with the dews of Heaven and to make the inhabitants of every denomination participate in the temporal and spiritual blessings of that people whose God is Jehovah.

G. Washington

To the Convention of the Universal Church

c.9 Aug. 1790

Gentlemen, I thank you cordially for the congratulations which you offer on my appointment to the office I have the honor to hold in the government of the United States.

It gives me the most sensible pleasure to find, that, in our nation, however different are the sentiments of citizens on religious doctrines, they generally concur in one thing, for their political professions and practices are almost universally friendly to the order and happiness of our civil institutions — I am also happy in finding this disposition particularly evinced by your society. It is moreover my earnest desire, that all the members of every association or community, throughout the United States, may make such use of the auspicious years of Peace, liberty and free enquiry, with which they are now favored, as they shall hereafter find occasion to rejoice for having done.

With great satisfaction I embrace this opportunity to express my acknowledgements for the interest my affectionate fellow-citizens have taken in my recovery from a late dangerous indisposition,[2] and I assure you, Gentlemen, that in mentioning my obligations for the effusions of your benevolent wishes on my behalf, I feel animated with new zeal, that my conduct may ever be worthy of your favorable opinion, as well as such as shall in every respect best comport with the character of an intelligent and accountable Being.

G. Washington

> To the Hebrew Congregation
> In Newport, Rhode Island
> Newport, R.I., 18 August 1790

Gentlemen While I receive, with much satisfaction, your Address replete with expressions of affection and esteem; I rejoice in the opportunity of assuring you, that I shall always retain a grateful remembrance of the cordial welcome I experienced in my visit to Newport, from all classes of Citizens.

The reflection on the days of difficulty and danger which are past is rendered the more sweet, from a consciousness that they are succeeded by days of uncommon prosperity and security. If we have wisdom to make the best use of the advantages with which we are now favored, we cannot fail, under the just administration of a good Government, to become a great and a happy people.

The Citizens of the United States of America have a right to applaud themselves for having given to mankind examples of an enlarged and liberal policy: a policy worthy of imitation. All possess alike liberty of conscience and immunities of citizenship. It is now no more that toleration is spoken of, as if it was by the indulgence of one class of people, that another enjoyed the exercise of their inherent natural rights. For happily the Government of the United States, which gives to bigotry no sanction, to persecution no assistance requires only that they who live under its protection should demean themselves as good citizens, in giving it on all occasions their effectual support.

It would be inconsistent with the frankness of my character not to avow that I am pleased with your favorable opinion of my Administration, and fervent wishes for my felicity. May the Children of the Stock of Abraham, who dwell in this land, continue to merit and enjoy the good will of the other Inhabitants; while every one shall sit in safety under his own vine and fig tree, and there shall be none to make him afraid. May the father of all mercies scatter light and not darkness in our paths, and make us all in our several vocations useful here, and in his own due time and way everlastingly happy.

G: Washington

To the Hebrew Congregations of
Philadelphia, New York, Charleston, and Richmond

Philadelphia, 13 December 1790

Gentlemen, The liberality of sentiment toward each other which marks every political and religious denomination of men in this Country, stands unparalleled in the history of Nations. The affection of such people is a treasure beyond the reach of calculation; and the repeated proofs which my fellow Citizens have given of their attachment to me, and approbation of my doings form the purest source of my temporal felicity. The affectionate expressions of your address again excite my gratitude, and receive my warmest acknowledgments.

The Power and Goodness of the Almighty were strongly Manifested in the events of our late glorious revolution; and his kind interposition in our behalf has been no less visible in the establishment of our present equal government. In war he directed the Sword; and in peace he has ruled in our Councils. My agency in both has been guided by the best intentions, and a sense of the duty which I owe my Country: and as my exertions have hitherto been amply rewarded by the Approbation of my fellow Citizens, I shall endeavour to deserve a continuance of it by my future conduct.

May the same temporal and eternal blessings which you implore for me, rest upon your Congregations.

G. Washington

The following letter includes Washington's important and now famous pronouncement that in America "every person may here worship God according to the dictates of his own heart." The original document is in the Pennsylvania Historical Society.

To the New Church In Baltimore, Maryland
c.27 January 1793

Gentlemen It has ever been my pride to merit the approbation of my fellow citizens, by a faithful and honest discharge of the duties annexed to those stations in which they have been pleased to place me; and the dearest rewards of my services have been those testimonies of esteem and confidence with which they have honored me. But to the manifest interposition of an over-ruling Providence, and to the patriotic exertions of united America, are to be ascribed those events which have given us a respectable rank among the nations of the Earth.

We have abundant reason to rejoice, that in this land the light of truth and reason have triumphed over the power of bigotry and superstition, and that every person may here worship God according to the dictates of his own heart. In this enlightened age and in this land of equal liberty, it is our boast, that a man's religious tenets will not forfeit the protection of the laws, nor deprive him of the right of attaining and holding the highest offices that are known in the United States.

Your prayers for my present and future felicity are received with gratitude; and I sincerely wish, Gentlemen, that you may in your social and individual capacities taste those blessings, which a gracious God bestows upon the righteous.

Go: Washington

Well-wishers from across the country, including many churches, wrote Washington when he retired from the presidency in 1797 after two terms in office. The two letters that follow are Washington's replies to addresses from the Episcopal Churches and from the Protestant Clergy of Philadelphia. The first letter is in the David Library of the American Revolution at Washington Crossing, Pennsylvania, and the second survives in letter-book form in the Washington Papers at the Library of Congress.

> To the Philadelphia Episcopal Churches
> c.2 March 1797

Gentlemen, To this public testimony of your approbation of my conduct & affection for my person, I am not insensible; and your prayers for my present and future happiness, merit my warmest acknowledgments. It is with peculiar satisfaction I can say, that, prompted by a high sense of duty in my attendance on public worship, I have been gratified, during my residence among you, by the liberal and interesting discourses which have been delivered in your churches.

Believing that that Government alone can be approved by Heaven, which promotes peace and secures protection to its Citizens in everything that is dear and interesting to them; it has been the great object of my Administration to insure those valuable ends: And when, to a consciousness of the purity of my intentions, is added the approbation of my fellow citizens, I shall experience in my retirement that heartfelt satisfaction, which can only be exceeded by the hope of future happiness.

Go: Washington

To the Philadelphia Protestant Clergy
Philadelphia, c.3 March 1797

Gentlemen, Not to acknowledge with gratitude and sensibility the affectionate addresses and benevolent wishes of my fellow Citizens on my retiring from public life, would prove that I have been unworthy of the confidence which they have been pleased to repose in me.

And, among these public testimonies of attachment and approbation none can be more grateful than that of so respectable a body as your's.

Beleiving, as I do, that *Religion* and *morality* are the essential pillars of civic society, I view, with unspeakable pleasure, that harmony and Brotherly Love which characterizes the clergy of different denominations — as well in this, as in other parts of the United States; exhibiting to the world a new and interesting spectacle, at once the pride of our Country and the surest basis of universal Harmony.

That your Labours for the good of mankind may be crowned with success — that your temporal enjoyments may be commensurate with your merits — and that the future reward of good and faithful servants may be your's, I shall not cease to supplicate the Divine Author of life and felicity.

Go: Washington

Washington's step-granddaughter Eleanor (Nelly) Parke Custis Lewis wrote the following letter to Jared Sparks, the American historian, clergyman, and president of Harvard College, in 1833. Sparks, who was the first to edit Washington's writings, had requested information about Washington's religious beliefs for his book, The Life of Washington. *The Valley Forge Historical Society owns the original letter. Note that Nelly says she never witnessed Washington's private devotions.*

Nelly Custis Lewis to Jared Sparks
Woodlawn, 26 February, 1833

Sir, I received your favor of the 20th instant last evening, and hasten to give you the information, which you desire.

Truro Parish is the one in which Mount Vernon, Pohick Church, and Woodlawn are situated. Fairfax Parish is now Alexandria. Before the Federal District was ceded to Congress, Alexandria was in Fairfax County. General Washington had a pew in Pohick Church, and one in Christ Church at Alexandria. He was very instrumental in establishing Pohick Church, and I believe subscribed largely. His pew was near the pulpit. I have a perfect recollection of being there, before his election to the presidency, with him and my grandmother. It was a beautiful church, and had a large, respectable, and wealthy congregation, who were regular attendants.

He attended the church at Alexandria, when the weather and roads permitted a ride of ten miles. In New York and Philadelphia he never omitted attendance at church in the morning, unless detained by indisposition. The afternoon was spent in his own room at home; the evening with his family, and without company. Sometimes an old and intimate friend called to see us for an hour or two; but visiting and visitors were prohibited for that day.

No one in church attended to the services with more reverential respect. My grandmother, who was eminently pious, never deviated from her early habits. She always knelt. The General, as was then the custom, stood during the devotional parts of the service. On communion Sundays, he left the church with me, after the blessing, and returned home, and we sent the carriage back for my grandmother.

It was his custom to retire to his library at nine or ten o'clock, where he remained an hour before he went to his chamber. He always rose before the sun, and remained in his library until called to breakfasdt [sic]. I never witnessed his private devotions. I never inquired about them. I should have thought it the greatest heresy to doubt his firm belief in Christianity. His life, his writings, prove that he was a Christian. He was not one of those who act or pray, "that they may be seen of men." He communed with his God in secret.

My mother resided two years at Mount Vernon, after her marriage with John Parke Custis, the only son of Mrs. Washington. I have heard her say that General Washington always received the sacrament with my grandmother before the revolution. When my aunt, Miss Custis, died suddenly at Mount Vernon, before they could realize the event, he knelt by her and prayed most fervently, most affectingly, for her recovery. Of this I was assured by Judge Washington's mother, and other witnesses.

He was a silent, thoughtful man. He spoke little generally; never of himself. I never heard him relate a single act of his life during the war I have often seen him perfectly abstracted, his lips moving, but no sound was perceptible. I have sometimes made him laugh most heartily from sympathy with my joyous and extravagant spirits. I was probably one of the last persons on earth to whom he would have addressed serious conversation, particularly when he knew that I had the most perfect model of female excellence ever with me as my monitress, who acted the part of a tender and devoted parent, loving me as only a mother can love, and never extenuating or approving in me what she disapproved in others.

She never omitted her private devotions, or her public duties; and she and her husband were so perfectly united and happy, that he must have been a Christian. She had no doubts, no fears for him. After forty years of devoted affection and uninterrupted happiness, she resigned him without a murmur into the arms of his Savior and his God, with the assured hope of his eternal felicity. Is it necessary that any one should certify, "General Washington avowed himself to me a believer in Christianity?" As well may we question his patriotism, his heroic, disinterested devotion to his country. His mottos were, "Deeds, not Words"; and, "For God and my Country." With sentiments of esteem, I am, &c.

Religion and George Washington 51

George Washington's Prayer Book

On April 21, 22, 23, 1891, there was sold at the auction rooms of Thomas Birch's Sons, 1110 Chestnut Street, Philadelphia, a collection of Washington relics owned by Washington descendants Lawrence Washington, Bushrod C. Washington, Thomas B. Washington, and J. R. C. Lewis. Included in the sale was "The Daily Sacrifice," a twenty-four page manuscript document written in a pocket memorandum book and subsequently circulated as "Washington's Prayers," "Washington's Prayer Book," or "Washington's Prayer Journal." The catalog of the sale was prepared by Philadelphia auctioneer Stan. V. Henkels, who asserted that the manuscript was not only in Washington's own handwriting, written when the future Father of His Country was about twenty years of age, but that Washington even composed the prayers himself. Both claims are patently false. The prayer book had been among a group of papers already rejected by the Smithsonian Institute as having no value, and at the time of the sale others continued to challenge its authenticity. Tens of thousands of genuine Washington manuscripts have survived to the present, including many from the youthful Washington, and even a cursory comparison of the prayer book with a genuine Washington manuscript reveals that they are not the same handwriting. (See illustrations.) Nevertheless, the prayers continue to be disseminated under Washington's name, thanks to their publication in the early twentieth century by William Herbert Burk (1867–1933) as *Washington's Prayers* (Norristown, Pennsylvania, 1907) and later republication by William Jackson Johnstone (1867–1933) in *George Washington The Christian* (New York and Cincinnati, 1919). What follows is Burk's original publication, *Washington's Prayers,* which contains Burk's introductory essay as well as facsimile images and his transcription of the prayers. It is hoped that this republication of Burk's work with the facsimiles will help to dispel the notion that the manuscript of the prayers are in Washington's own handwriting.

Washington's handwriting at age 20, from his Barbados Diary

(Library of Congress)

54   The Ways of Providence

*The Sea greatly [...]
changed our course to
other Tack*

*Monday 6th. Last night the Wind
varied to the S'ward and grew calm
at 6 AM freshned and had got to
West we made another tack and
stood N'N'W. this day Warm & pleasant*

*Tuesday 7th.
Wind fresh & Wav-
ing with some Squalls & rough
Sea*

*Wednesday 8th. About 2 this morn-
ing the Wind died away and at*

Another page of Washington's Barbados Diary

(Library of Congress)

Note the handwriting of the "Daily Sacrifice" manuscript

Washington Memorial Chapel at Valley Forge, Pennsylvania

(from an old postcard)

The chapel, completed in 1917, was the inspiration of W. Herbert Burk, an Episcopal minister and long-time defender of the role of religion in George Washington's life

WASHINGTON'S PRAYERS

BY

W. HERBERT BURK, B.D.

Rector of All Saints' Church, Norristown, and Minister-in-Charge of the Washington Memorial Chapel, Valley Forge; Member of the Historical Society of Pennsylvania; Author of the "Historical and Topographical Guide to Valley Forge."

———

PUBLISHED FOR THE BENEFIT OF THE

WASHINGTON MEMORIAL CHAPEL

———

NORRISTOWN, PA.

1907

Five hundred copies of this Book have been printed, of which this is

No. 116

PREFACE.

THE following account of Washington's Prayers was read before the Clerical Brotherhood of the Diocese of Pennsylvania, May 13, 1907. Its publication was then urged on the ground that it was a contribution to the understanding of the character of Washington. If this be true, even in the smallest degree, it belongs to the American people, whose appreciation of Washington, having passed through the stages of adulation and detraction, is now becoming both sane and just.

To Mr. Stan V. Henkels, of Philadelphia, I am indebted for permission to reprint the facsimile of "The Daily Sacrifice."

W. HERBERT BURK.

All Saints' Rectory,
    December 2, 1907.

WASHINGTON'S PRAYERS
By Herbert Burk

THE story of Washington's prayer at Valley Forge is familiar to all Americans. It is woven into the web and woof of the historic tapestry of the school-child mind, illuminated by the well-known picture of the scene painted by Henry Brueckner. But this hangs by itself. There is no companion piece. So far as most Americans know, that prayer was the result of the direst need, and not the evidence of a constant practice, or of a deep-seated principle of worship. Prayerfulness is not an element in the character of "The True George Washington" as portrayed by Paul Leicester Ford, although that writer had the greatest opportunity for studying this side of Washington's character. Without the due appreciation of Washington's prayerful spirit I believe no one can really understand the man. Of that spirit we have ample proof in the testimony of those who knew him in the flesh and in the testimony of his own letters and official documents.

The prayer at Valley Forge was not an isolated act, unrelated to the rest of his life. Best known, perhaps, of his acts of devotion this but illuminates the others less understood, and turns our eyes to the man's secret source of strength, hopefulness, confidence and sincerity. Thus it was understood by Bishop Gibson, who in the course of his sermon at the first service in the Washington Memorial Chapel at Valley Forge on "The Glory of Valley Forge" said:

We thank thee, O good Quaker brother, Isaac Potts, that, whether led by curiosity or anxiety, thou didst follow the General to the woods near yonder house, his headquarters, and heard his strong, quiet voice in the accents of prayer under the trees! We would not have had that happen often, but a single approach, even to another's sanctuary, may be excused. Its effect in this case is rarely illuminating. We understand a great many things. Now we know the meaning of the entry in his diary made in 1774: "Williamsburg, June 1st. Went to Church and fasted all day." Now we know what to think of his Church attendance. Now we can feel, as Bishop Meade says his family felt, about his taking his candle every night at nine o'clock and going to his study to remain until ten. Now we can understand his active concern in the affairs of his parish and his insistence on the service of a chaplain for his men, and his frequent references to Divine Providence. The sun, streaming through one mullioned window of the noble library, floods the apartment with light, and shows where each volume stands on its well ordered shelves.

We must think that Washington was a man of prayer, of the habit of prayer; and few thoughtful people, I dare assert, will fail to find in this fact the secret of his power over himself.

Religion and George Washington

By the side of the young Quaker preacher's discovery at Valley Forge we must place those made by his companions in arms and the members of his household if we would rightly measure the man. During the French and Indian War, Colonel Temple of Virginia, on unexpected visits to the marquee of Washington, "more than once found him on his knees at his devotions." The tent made for his use during the War of the Revolution was divided into two sections, the inner one providing a more private apartment. This was his usual place of prayer. The leafy bower might be used at times, but like the library at Mount Vernon, this was his real sanctuary. Here General Porterfield found him "on his knees at his morning devotions."

Washington's adopted daughter, Eleanor Parke Custis, in a letter to Jared Sparks describing her father's attitude toward religion, said: "It was his custom to retire to his library at nine or ten o'clock, where he remained an hour before he went to his chamber. He always rose before the sun, and remained in his library until called to breakfast. I never *witnessed* his private devotions. I never *inquired* about them. I should have thought it the greatest heresy to doubt his firm belief in Christianity. His life, his writings, prove that he was a Christian. He was not one of those who act or pray, 'that they may be seen of men.' He communed with his God in secret."

What Eleanor Parke Custis did not see, Robert Lewis, Washington's nephew and private secretary, did see. In 1827 he told Mr. Sparks that "he had accidentally witnessed his private devotions in his library both morning and evening; that on these occasions he had seen him in a kneeling posture with a

Bible open before him, and that he believed such to have been his daily practice. . . . He added that it was the President's custom to go to his library in the morning at four o'clock, and that, after his devotions, he usually spent his time till breakfast in writing letters."

What form his devotions assumed we cannot tell. As the son of Mary Washington, and as a churchman, he was familiar with the Book of Common Prayer, its daily services and forms of devotion. In his library were Bibles, including Wilson's, which he describes in willing it to "the Reverend, now Bryan Lord Fairfax," as "a Bible in three folio volumes with notes, presented to me by the Right Reverend Thomas Wilson, Bishop of Sodor and Man," one Prayer Book, at least, Thomas Comber's "Discourses upon Common Prayer," and volumes of sermons. The "Discourses upon Common Prayer" is now in the Boston Athenæum, and contains the autographs of Augustine Washington, Mary Washington and George Washington.

From his mother Washington received his earliest religious training. That this was conscientiously given no one can doubt. That it followed the lines of the Prayer Book is both natural and evident. "Not only do his public and private papers show the fervency and constancy of his devotions have been attested, and that he respected his mother's early injunction never to forget his private prayers." For him the Prayer Book's use was not confined to the parish church or to the library at Mount Vernon. It was his companion at Great Meadows as well as at Pohick or Alexandria, and he who in his last hour said, "I die hard, but I am not afraid to die" had committed the body of the brave Braddock to

Religion and George Washington

the grave with the triumphant words of our beautiful Office for the Burial of the Dead. Trained as a child in the use of the Prayer Book the words of its prayers were more familiar to Washington than any others, and public and private use made them in a real sense, we may well believe, "Washington's Prayers."

But it is not my purpose to dwell upon this fact, important as it is to the true understanding of the character of Washington. The influence of the Prayer Book upon his life and his relation to its services while never fully treated have been considered. The Prayer Book was his heritage by birth and its atmosphere formed a part of his natural environment. it played its part, and an important part, in the making of the man. Its forms gave dignity to his language and strengthened his sense of order. Its services formed no small part of his education and did their share in refining his tastes. But, to my mind, their greatest office was spiritual. They developed in him the spirit of worship and made him truly a man of prayer. They taught him to hold communion with God, this "Unexpressive man, whose life expressed so much."

When Washington was thirteen years of age he copied some verses on "Christmas Day," beginning:

> "Assist me, Muse divine, to sing the morn,
> On which the Saviour of mankind was born."

Between that age and sixteen he copied or wrote his "Rules of Behaviour in Company and Conversation," the most famous of which is: "Labor to keep alive in your breast that little spark of celestial fire, *Conscience*." At seventeen he recorded in his mother's Bible the date of his birth and baptism. At twenty-three he officiated at the burial of Braddock. At twenty-six he wrote to the President of the Council: "The last Assembly, in their supply Bill, provided for a chaplain for our regiment, for whom I had often very unsuccessfully applied to Governor Dinwiddie. I can now flatter myself, that your Honour will be pleased to appoint a sober, serious man for this duty. Common decency, Sir, in a camp calls for the services of a divine, and which ought not to be dispensed with, altho' the world should be so uncharitable as to think us void of religion, and incapable of good instructions."

I call attention to these facts and dates because they have an important bearing upon one of the most interesting documents connected with the name of Washington.

On April 21, 22, 23, 1891, there was sold at the auction rooms of Thomas Birch's Sons, 1110 Chestnut Street, Philadelphia, a remarkable collection of Washington relics owned by Lawrence Washington, Bushrod C. Washington, Thos. B. Washington and J. R. C. Lewis. Lot No. 250 is thus described in the catalogue of the sale prepared by Mr. Stan. V. Henkels, one of the greatest authorities on Washingtoniana: "GEN'L GEO. WASHINGTON'S MANUSCRIPT PRAYER BOOK, entitled the 'Daily Sacrifice.' For Sunday Morning, Sunday Evening, Monday Morning, Monday Evening, Tuesday Morning, Tuesday

Religion and George Washington

Evening, Wednesday Morning, Wednesday Evening and Thursday Morning. *Small 12mo, 24 pages."*

"This gem is all in the handwriting of Geo. Washington, when about twenty years old, and is, without exception, the most hallowed of all his writings. It is neatly written on twenty-four pages of a little book about the size of the ordinary pocket memorandum. We quote the prayer for Sunday morning:

> Almighty God, and most merciful Father, who didst command the children of Israel, to offer a daily sacrifice to thee, that thereby they might glorify and praise thee for thy protection, both night and day; receive, O Lord, my morning sacrifice which I now offer to thee; I yield thee humble and hearty thanks, that thou has't preserved me from the dangers of the night passed, and brought me to the light of this day, and the comforts thereof, a day which is consecrated to thine own service, and for thine honour. Let my heart, therefor, gracious God, be so affected with the glory and majesty of it, that I may not do mine own works but wait on thee, and discharge those weighty duties, thou requirest of me; and since thou are a God of pure eyes, and wilt be sanctified in all who draw near unto thee, who dost not regard the sacrifice of fools, nor hear sinners who tread in thy courts, pardon I beseech thee, my sins, remove them from thy presence, as far as the east is from the west; and accept of me

for the merits of thy Son Jesus Christ, that when I come into thy temple, and compass thine Altar, my prayer may come before thee as incense, and as I desire thou wouldst hear me calling upon thee in my prayers, so give me grace to hear thee calling on me in thy word, that it may be wisdom, righteousness, reconciliation, and peace to the saving of my soul on the day of the Lord Jesus. Grant that I may hear it with reverence, receive it with meekness, mingle it with faith and, and that it may accomplish in me Gracious God, the good work for which thou hast sent it. Bless my family, kindred, friends and country; be our God and guide this day and forever, for his sake who laid down in the grave and rose again for us, Jesus Christ, Our Lord. Amen."

By the merest accident Mr. Henkels discovered this document. While making arrangements for the sale he came across a dilapidated trunk, which Mr. Washington assured him contained only papers of no value, papers which had been rejected by the authorities of the Smithsonian Institute when offered for exhibition. in looking them over he came across this document and recognized at once what he considered the penmanship of Washington. His judgment was substantiated by other experts, to whom the manuscript was submitted.

Mr. W. E. Benjamin, the well-known New York dealer, purchased the manuscript for twelve hundred and fifty dollars, and by him it was sold to the late Reverend Charles Frederick Hoffman, D.D. Naturally the discovery and sale of such an important manuscript of Washington attracted considerable attention and in the columns of the *New York Evening Post* the authenticity of the manuscript was challenged. It is not my purpose to revive that controver[s]y. Where experts disagree a layman's opinion counts for little. Able experts declare the prayers were written by Washington. One says they were written by a Washington. Another, they are "written in the unformed hand of the great patriot. It is a well-known fact that Washington between the years 1755 and 1763 changed his hand from the angular to the round formation."

The ultimate judgment must be based on the chirography, for there are no *a priori* arguments to prove that Washington did not write them. The facts set forth in these pages are such as to place the *onus probandi* on those who deny they are Washington's handiwork.

Lawrence Washington, who sold the manuscript in Philadelphia had inherited it with other Washington relics from his father, Col. John Augustine Washington, the last private owner of Mount Vernon. He had inherited them from his mother, Mrs. Jane C. Washington, who had inherited them from her husband, John Augustine Washington. He inherited them from Judge Bushrod Washington to whom they had been bequeathed by George Washington.

A reproduction of the manuscript was made and published by Mr. Henkels, and while it was in the possession of Mr. Benjamin it was again reproduced and published by the Beacon Publishing Company of New York.

What disposition Dr. Hoffman made of the manuscript I have been unable to discover. In Dr. Potter's "Washington a Model in his Library and Life" is the following statement: "The Rev. Dr. Chas. F. Hoffman has lately purchased 'Washington's Prayers,' the MSS. containing morning and evening prayers for various days of the week. He has under consideration, for the benefit of young men and others, a division of this very valuable manuscript, forming a sermon every page, for deposit in the fireproof libraries of St. Stephen's College, Hobart College, Trinity College, and the University of the South, each institution to have also a complete free circulation of the whole work."

An analysis of the first prayer shows that it is made up almost entirely of sentences from the Prayer Book, and the other prayers are drawn largely from the same source. Almost every part of the Prayer Book has been laid under contribution, showing that the author was very familiar with its entire contents.

While the Prayer Book is undoubtedly the source of the prayers, the question of their authorship is not determined. Dr. Lyman Abbott and Prof. Upham attributed them to Washington. In writing to the New York publishers, Dr. Abbott said: "An age whose virtues are philanthropic, whose defect is lack of spiritual perception, and whose characteristic vice is irreverence, can hardly fail to receive benefit from the publication of the prayers of one honored by men of all faiths, and even of none, as is George Washington. They may well seem to indicate that source of strength which sustained him with a divinely-inspired patience in an epoch in which mere enthusiasm of humanity, unnourished by secret springs of piety, must have dried up and utterly failed." Dr. S. F. Upham, Professor of Practical Theology in Drew Theological Seminary, wrote: "The 'Daily Prayers' of George Washington abound in earnest thought, expressed in simple, beautiful, fervent and evangelical language. They reveal to us the real life of the great patriot, and attest his piety. None can read those petitions, which bore his desires to God, and often brought answers of peace, without having a grader conception of Washington's character."

No proof can be given that these prayers were composed by Washington, but, on the other hand, no proof has been produced to show that they were not his work. Profes[s]or Lucien M. Robinson is of the opinion that they are taken from some collection of prayers, but has not yet been able to confirm his opinion. I think this is very probable, and have endeavored to discover their source, but so far the search has been in vain. At present, the question is an open one, and its settlement will depend on the discovery of the originals, or upon the demonstration that they are the work of Washington. There are no *a priori* grounds for the denial of his authorship. We have seen, from the facts and dates that I have submitted, that there was a decidedly marked interest in religious matters in the youthful Washington. I might have added that one of the earliest, if not the very earliest, signature of Washington is found in a volume of sermons, and that a good proportion of his books were religious in character.

That this interest fruited in prayer we have the evidence of those who knew him. Moreover, we know that his prayers were impressive. This is stated in the tradition of his discovery by Isaac Potts, and the tradition is substantiated by the fact that Washington, after pledging himself to remain in a tent, was prevailed upon to occupy the home of the Quaker preacher, which he did on Christmas Day, 1777. Another tradition, preserved by the family in whose home Washington made his headquarters before the engagement of Chatterton Hill, tells of his prayer before the battle. "On this occasion, his loyal heart, stung with the epithet of 'rebel' hurled at patriots, was, at the family altar, poured out in the language of the very 'Bible hero without a flaw' he is said to resemble. His words were those of the 22d verse of chapter xxii of the book of Joshua: 'The Lord, God of gods, the Lord God of gods, he knoweth, and Israel, he shall know; if it be rebellion, or if in transgression against the Lord.'"

It would be most interesting to prove that the prayers in the "Daily Sacrifice" were composed by Washington, or even that they were copied by him. But, if neither could be done, it would not affect our judgment of him as a man of prayer, for that does not depend upon this document. It is based on his unquestioned writings, and the judgment thus founded is illustrated and confirmed by the tradition of his prayers.

The first of these prayers to which I would call attention is found in a letter written on the 20th of July, 1758, near Fort Loudon. It is the prayer of Washington's romance — written by the young commander advancing in a dangerous campaign, written to her who had won his heart's love, Mrs. Martha Custis. The letter and prayer are as follows:

Religion and George Washington

July 20, 1758.

We have begun our march for the Ohio. A courier is starting for Williamsburg, and I embrace the opportunity to send a few words to one whose life is now inseparable from mine. Since that happy hour when we made our pledges to each other, my thoughts have been continually going to you as another Self. That an all-powerful Providence may keep us both in safety is the prayer of your ever faithful and affectionate friend.

I quote this letter in full because it illustrates the manner in which Washington made prayer a part of his correspondence. It is a type of the other prayers which I have collected from his writings. Helpless to protect her whom he loved, or to defend himself for her sake, he commits both to God's keeping. The prayer is brief, simple and comprehensive, but no one will doubt for a moment its reality or earnestness any more than did she who first read it, and afterwards preserved it.

The prayers which we will now consider belong to a much later period of Washington's life, but we may well believe that they were none the less real. Between this lover's prayer of his youth and those of the Commander in-Chief of the army of the United Colonies or of the first President of the Republic were long years. But in those years were experiences such as few men have to teach them of the nearness of God. I believe they deepened the fervor of his prayers. In a letter to General Armstrong, he said: "I am sure there never was a people, who had more reason to acknowledge a divine interposition in their affairs, than those of the United States; and I should be pained to believe that they have forgotten that agency, which was so often manifested during our revolution, or that they failed to consider the omnipotence of that God, who is alone able to protect them."

For the purpose of this paper I have divided these prayers into three classes, as follows:

    1. The Prayers for the Churches.

    2. The Prayers for Institutions, etc.

    3. The Prayers for the Nation.

PART I.

THE PRAYERS FOR THE CHURCHES.

DURING the year 1789, following his election to the presidency, Washington received addresses of congratulation and pledges of support from various bodies of citizens. Each of these was responded to in some fitting form, and in these responses are to be found much material for the consideration of any one who would attempt to form a true conception of his religious character. Several of these letters, like the one to Mrs. Martha Custis, end in a prayer. The letters to the churches were written during the years 1789 and 1790. of the thirteen letters which I have noted, eight contain prayers. Those containing prayers were addressed to the Protestant Episcopal Church, the Methodist,

Dutch Reformed, German Reformed, Roman Catholic, United Brethren, New Church and Jewish. Those without prayers were written to the German Lutheran and Congregational Churches, the Friends and Virginia Baptists.

Of those with prayers the weakest expressions are found in those written to the "German Reformed Congregations in the United States" and to the "Members of the New Church in Baltimore." In the letter to the former, he said: "May your devotions before the throne of grace be prevalent in calling down the blessings of Heaven upon yourselves and your country;" and in the letter to the latter: "Your prayers for my present and future felicity are received with gratitude; and I sincerely wish, gentlemen, that you may in your social and individual capacities taste those blessings, which a gracious God bestows upon the righteous."

If these stood by themselves they would hardly be noted as prayers, but would pass as mere pious wishes. When, however, they are considered in connection with the other prayers, we recognize that they, too, are real prayers, although weakly marked as such.

Four of the prayers are similar in purport and vary but little in expression. These are found in the letter to the Directors of the Society of the United Brethren, where he said: "I pray Almighty God to have you always in His holy keeping;" in that to the Synod of the Reformed Church, where the prayer is: "I beseech the Almighty to take you and yours under His special care;" in that to the Bishops of the Methodist Episcopal Church, where it is: "I likewise implore the divine benediction on your religious community;" and in his reply to the address of the General Convention of his own Church, in which is the following prayer: "May you and the people whom you represent, be the happy subjects of the divine benediction both here and hereafter."

The prayer in the letter to the Roman Catholics in the United States is colored by the special line of thought in his mind. In England the Romanists had long been subject to legal disability, but in 1778 steps were taken to give them civil rights. This stirred up the people throughout the country and resulted in riots, the most noted of which were the Lord George Riots of 1780. Washington, believing strongly in the freedom of religious thought, but willing to have a tax levied to support religion, wrote in December, 1780, expressing his hope that in America the Romanists would receive justice and liberality, and that Americans would gratefully remember the part which was taken in the Revolution by the Romanists of America and of France. In view of these facts the prayer becomes significant. He said: "And may the members of your society in America, animated alone by the pure spirit of Christianity, and still conducting themselves as the faithful subjects of our free government, enjoy every temporal and spiritual felicity."

By the side of this prayer we must place that in the letter to the Hebrew Congregation in the city of Savannah. After expressing the hope that the Jews would be benefited by the spirit of liberality which prevailed, his prayer was: "May the same wonder-working Deity, who long since delivered the Hebrews from their Egyptian oppressors, and planted them in the promised land, whose providential agency has lately been conspicuous in establishing these United States as an independent nation, still continue to water them with the dews of Heaven, and to make the inhabitants of every denomination participate in the temporal and spiritual blessing of that people, whose God is Jehovah."

Let me add to this series of prayers one which seems to be its natural climax. It is found in a letter written on his retirement from the Presidency to the "Clergy of Different Denominations, residing in and near the city of Philadelphia." "That your labors for the good of mankind may be crowned with success, that your temporal enjoyments may be commensurate with your merits, and that the future reward of good and faithful servants may be yours, I shall not cease to supplicate the Divine Author of life and felicity."

PART II.

THE PRAYERS FOR INSTITUTIONS, ETC.

UNDER this head I have grouped prayers for colleges, societies, towns and States. Naturally, these vary greatly in character and expression. To the Board of Trustees of Dartmouth College, he said: "That your labors may be crowned with success, and render you happy in its consequences, is my sincere prayer." He closed a letter to the Society of the Cincinnati with these words: "To the most affectionate wishes for your temporal happiness, I add a fervent prayer for your eternal felicity;" and in a letter to the Grand Lodge of Free and

Accepted Masons of Massachusetts he said: "I sincerely pray that the Great Architect of the Universe may bless you here, and receive you hereafter into His immortal temple." From among the prayers for towns I take this for Portsmouth, New Hampshire: "I earnestly pray that the Great Ruler of the Universe may smile upon your honest exertions here, and reward your well-doing with future happiness."

The addresses of the legislatures of the States, both upon his election to the Presidency and also upon his retirement from service were answered by Washington in fitting acknowledgements. Like the letters to the churches, some are without prayers. Of the prayers, I will reproduce only two. That for Connecticut follows congratulations upon the prospect of an abundant harvest, and is as follows: "May industry like theirs (the citizens of Connecticut) ever receive its reward, and may the smile of Heaven crown all endeavours, which are promoted by virtue, among which it is but justice to estimate your assurance of supporting our equal government."

In his answer to an address from the General Assembly of Massachusetts Washington utters the following comprehensive prayer:

> May that Being who is powerful to save, and in whose hands is the fate of nations, look down with an eye of tender pity and compassion upon the whole of the United Colonies; may He continue to smile upon their counsels and arms, and crown them with success, whilst employed in the cause of

virtue and mankind. May this distressed colony and its capital and every part of the wide extended continent, through His divine favour, be restored to more than their former lustre and once happy state, and have peace, liberty and safety secured upon a solid, permanent and lasting foundation.

PART III.

THE PRAYERS FOR THE NATION.

WASHINGTON'S Prayer Book training had made prayers for the nation a matter of course for him. They formed a part of the regular order of worship, and, therefore, it is no surprise to find him, when called to the work of building a new nation, uttering prayers for its guidance and welfare.

The Farewell Address, so familiar to all Americans, has, to a large extent, eclipsed an earlier document of a similar character, which was popularly known as "Washington's Legacy." It was a circular letter to the governors of all the States, and was written at Newburg, on the 8th of June, 1783. It concludes with this noble prayer: "I now make it my earnest prayer, that God would have you, and the State over which you preside, in His holy protection: that He would incline the hearts of the citizens to cultivate a spirit of subordination and obedience to government; to entertain a brotherly affection and love for one another, for their fellow citizens of the United States at large, and particularly for their brethren who have served in the field; and finally, that

He would most graciously be pleased to dispose us all to do justice, to love mercy, and to demean ourselves with that charity, humility and pacific temper of mind, which were the characteristics of the Divine Author of our blessed religion, and without an humble imitation of whose example in these things, we can never hope to be a happy nation."

The retirement to which he then looked, and in the shade of which he pledged himself to "implore the Divine benediction" on his Country, was very brief. Once more he was called to the leadership of the American people, and on April 30, 1789, he made his inaugural speech as President of the United States to both houses of Congress. To him it was a most solemn occasion. He concluded that speech with these words:

> Having thus imparted to you my sentiments, as they have been awakened by the occasion which brings us together, I shall take my present leave; but not without resorting once more to the benign Parent of the human race, in humble supplication, that, since He has been pleased to favor the American people with opportunities for deliberating in perfect tranqui[li]ty, and dispositions for deciding with unparalleled unanimity on a form of government for the security of their union and the advancement of their happiness; so His divine blessing may be equally *conspicuous* in the enlarged views, temperate consultations and the wise

measures on which the success of this government must depend.

In his second inaugural speech he said: "I have obeyed the suffrage, which commanded me to resume the executive power; and I humbly implore that Being, on whose will the fate of nations depends, to crown with success our mutual endeavours for the general happiness."

When De Kalb first met Washington he was sadly disappointed in him. But, as he soon learned, it was because he mistook the Commander-in-Chief's diffidence for weakness and incapacity. The only prayer in the Farewell Address is for the defense of his Country from the evil effects of his errors. He said: "Though in reviewing the incidents of my administration I am unconscious of intentional error, I am, nevertheless, too sensible of my defects not to think it probable that I have committed many errors. Whatever they may be, I fervently beseech the Almighty to avert or mitigate the evils to which they may tend."

Of all his prayers for our Country I like best that which I have had placed in the windows of the porch of the Washington Memorial Chapel at Valley Forge. In it his patriotism glows with his heart's love and his faith in God is deep and true. Had Washington written no other prayer, this would have been enough to reveal his religious nature.

"I commend the interests of our dearest country to the protection of Almighty God, and those who have the superintendence of them to His holy keeping."

To many it will be a matter of surprise that in none of these prayers does the name of Jesus appear. This does not mean that Washington was a Theist. He acknowledged Christ as the "Divine author of our blessed religion." There is another reason for the omission.

Washington's life was bounded by the eighteenth century. He must be judged therefore by the standards of the eighteenth century and not by those of the nineteenth or twentieth. The formative period of his life synchronized with that in which "the dullness of spiritual religion in the Church of England was slowly chilling into death," to use an expression of Wakeman. That writer's apology for the apathy of the clergy of the period is this: "If the coal from off the altar did not touch their lips, if the sword of the spirit did not pierce their hearts, if the power of the Cross was not dominant in their lives, it was because these are the special gifts and rewards of 'enthusiasm' and to be an 'enthusiast' in the eighteenth century was to be out of harmony with the age."

What was true of England was true of America. There had been the Great Awakening, but that was followed by a period of langour and the effects of the first Oxford movement were not felt in this country until the period of the Revolution. Consequently Washington's religious life was not marked by "enthusiasm." The effect of the age is seen in the avoidance of the more personal names of God. But the more one knows of the age the more remarkable does the religious life of Washington appear. These prayers reveal a deeply religious mind. Many of them are full of suppressed feeling. Nor can we doubt that they passed the supreme test of prayer — acceptance with God, for they expressed the heart's desire of one who, whatever his faults and failings were, in private life or public service, amid many temptations in trials and successes, strove always "to love mercy, and to walk humbly" with his God.

THE DAILY SACRIFICE

FAC-SIMILE

OF

Manuscript Prayer-Book

WRITTEN BY

GEORGE WASHINGTON

―――

First Published by Stan. V. Henkels,
Philadelphia, 1891

PHILADELPHIA, Oct. 30, 1907.

REV. W. HERBERT BURK.

My Dear Sir:

It gives me pleasure to allow you to reprint the facsimile of the Washington Prayers, and whatever benefit the copyright may confer on me I cheerfully transfer to you. We must all join hands to perpetuate the memory of him who stand alone in this country, Geo. Washington, the greatest of all men of his day, of our day and forever.

God bless you. I wish you luck. Yours sincerely,

STAN. V. HENKELS.

"Daily Sacrifice," page 1

The Ways of Providence

...d, that I may not do mine own works, but wait on Thee, and discharge those weighty duties Thou requirest of me; and since Thou art a God of pure eyes, and wilt be sanctified in all who draw near unto Thee, who dost not regard the sacrifice of fools, nor hear sinners who tread in thy courts, pardon I beseech thee, my sins, remove them from thy presence, as far as the east is from the west; and accept of me for the merits of thy son Jesus Christ, that when I come into thy temple, and compass thine altar, my prayer may come before thee as incense. And as I desire thou wouldst hear me calling upon thee in my prayers, so give me grace to hear thee calling on me in thy word, that...

"Daily Sacrifice," page 2

"Daily Sacrifice," page 3

> and imperfect performance of the duties of this day. I have called on thee for pardon and forgiveness of sins, but so coldly & carelessly that my prayers are become my sin and stand in need of pardon. I have heard thy holy word, but with such deadness of spirit that I have been an unprofitable and forgetful hearer, so that O Lord, tho' I have done thy work, yet it hath been so negligent that I may rather expect a curse than a blessing from thee. But O God, who art rich in mercy and plenteous in redemption, mark not I beseech thee what I have done amiss, remember

"Daily Sacrifice," page 4

Religion and George Washington

"Daily Sacrifice," page 5

standing, and help me thoroughly to examine myself concerning my knowledge, faith, and repentance. increase my faith, and direct me to the true object Jesus Christ the way, the truth, and the life. Bless O Lord all the people of this land, from the highest to the lowest. particularly those whom thou hast appointed to rule over us in church & states continue thy goodness to me this night. These weak petitions I humbly implore thee to hear accept & ans for the sake of thy Dear son Jesus Christ our Lord. amen

Monday morning
O eternal and everlasting God, I presume to present myself this morning before thy divine majesty, beseeching thee to accept of my hum

"Daily Sacrifice," page 6

Religion and George Washington

"Daily Sacrifice," page 7

> of the gospel; give me repentance
> from dead works; pardon my wander-
> ings, & direct my thoughts unto thy-
> self, the God of my salvation;
> teach me how to live in thy fear,
> labour in thy service, and ever to
> run in the ways of thy command-
> ments; make me always watchful
> over my heart, that neither the
> terrors of conscience, the loath-
> ing of holy duties, the love of sin,
> nor an unwillingness to depart
> this life, may cast me into a
> spiritual slumber, but daily
> frame me more & more into the
> likeness of thy son Jesus Christ,
> that living in thy fear, and dy-
> ing in thy favour, I may in thy
> appointed time attain the re-

"Daily Sacrifice," page 8

"Daily Sacrifice," page 9

> of thy own hand; thou gavest thy
> Son to die for me; and hast given
> me assurance of salvation, upon my
> repentance: and sincerely endea-
> vouring to conform my life to his
> holy precepts and example. Thou
> art pleased to lengthen out to me
> the time of repentance, and to move
> me to it by thy spirit and by thy word,
> by thy mercies, and by thy judgments.
> Out of a deepness of thy mercies and my
> own unworthiness, I do appear before
> at this time; I have sinned and
> done very wickedly, be merciful to
> me O God, and pardon me for Jesus
> Christ sake; instruct me in the
> particulars of my duty, and suffer
> me not to be tempted above what
> thou givest me strength to bear
> take care & I pray thee of my

"Daily Sacrifice," page 10

"Daily Sacrifice," page 11

"Daily Sacrifice," page 12

> Tuesday morning
> O Lord our God, most mighty and merciful father, I thine unworthy creature and servant do once more approach thy presence. Though not worthy to appear before thee, because of my natural corruptions, and the many sins and transgressions which I have committed against thy divine majesty; yet I beseech thee, for the sake of him in whom thou art well pleased, the Lord Jesus Christ, to admit me to render thee deserved thanks and praises for thy manifold mercies extended toward me, for the quiet rest & repose of the past night, for food, raiment, health, peace, liberty and the hopes of a better life through the

"Daily Sacrifice," page 13

merit of thy dear son's bitter passion. And oh kind father continue thy mercy and favour to me this day and ever hereafter, prosper all my lawful undertakings, let me have all my directions from thy holy spirit and success from thy bountiful hand. Let the bright beams of thy light so shine into my heart, and enlighten my mind in understanding thy blessed word, that I may be enabled to perform thy will in all things and effectually resist all temptations of the world, the flesh, and the devil. Preserve and defend our rulers in Church & state. Bless the people of this land, be a Father to the fatherless

"Daily Sacrifice," page 14

"Daily Sacrifice," page 15

> and iniquities I heap up against thee. If I should cast up the account of my good deeds done this day, how few and small would they be; but if I should reckon my miscarriages, surely they would be many and great. O blessed Father let thy son's blood wash me from all impurities, and cleanse me from the stains of sin that are upon me, Give me grace to lay hold upon his merits, that they may be my reconciliation and atonement unto thee,—That I may know my sins are forgiven by his death & Passion, embrace me in the arms of thy mercy; vouchsafe to receive me into the bosom of thy love, shadow me with thy wings that I may safely rest under thy protection this night;

"Daily Sacrifice," page 16

"Daily Sacrifice," page 17

"Daily Sacrifice," page 18

and before thee, in thought, word & deed: I have contemned thy majesty and holy laws. I have likewise sinned by omitting what I ought to have done, and committing what I ought not. I have rebelled against light, despised thy mercies and judgments, and broken my vows and promises; I have neglected the means of Grace, and opportunities of becoming better. my iniquities are multiplied and my sins are very great. I confess them O Lord, with shame and sorrow, detestation and loathing and desire to be vile in my own eyes, as I have rendered myself vile in thine. I humbly beseech thee to be merciful to me in the free pardon of my sins, for the sake of thy dear Son, my only saviour J. C. who came not to call the righteous, but sinners to repentance; be pleased to

"Daily Sacrifice," page 19

> renew my nature, and write
> thy laws upon my heart, and
> help me to live righteously, sober-
> ly and godly in this evil world;
> make me humble, meek, patient
> and contented, and work in me
> the grace of thy holy spirit.
> Prepare me for death and
> judgment, and let the thoughts
> thereof awaken me to a greater
> care and study to approve my-
> self unto thee in well doing.
> Bless our rulers in Church &
> State. Help all in affliction
> or adversity. Give them patience
> and a sanctified use of their
> affliction, and in thy good
> time deliverance from them.
> Forgive my enemies, take me
> into thy protection this day,
> keep me in perfect peace,
> which I ask in the name
> & for the sake of Jesus —

"Daily Sacrifice," page 20

"Daily Sacrifice," page 21

> and my infirmaties & wants call for a continuance of thy tender mercies. cleanse my soul, O Lord I beseech thee, from whatever is offensive to thee and hurtful to me, and give me what is convenient for me. watch over me this night, and give me comfortable and sweet sleep to fit me for the service of the day following. Let my soul watch for the coming of the Lord Jesus; let my bed put me in mind of my grave, and my rising from thence of my last resurrection; O heavenly Father, so frame this heart of mine, that I may ever delight to live according to thy will and command, in

"Daily Sacrifice," page 22

"Daily Sacrifice," page 23

> those most holy words of earthly
> pray our Father &c..
>
> ---
>
> Thursday morning
> Most gracious Lord God, whose
> dwelling is in the highest heavens,
> and yet beholdest the lowly and
> humble upon earth. I blush and
> am ashamed to lift up my eyes
> to thy dwelling place, because
> I have sinned against thee;
> look down, I beseech thee, upon
> me, thy unworthy servant who
> prostrate myself at the
> of thy mercy, confessing my own
> unworthiness, and beseech pardon
> for my sins; what couldst thou
> have done Lord more for me, or
> what could I have done more
> against thee? Thou didst send
> thy Son to take our nature

"Daily Sacrifice," page 24

A TRANSCRIPT OF
"THE DAILY SACRIFICE"
THE DAILY SACRIFICE.

SUNDAY MORNING.

ALMIGHTY GOD, and most merciful father, who didst command the children of Israel to offer a daily sacrifice to Thee, that thereby they might glorify and praise thee for thy protection both night and day; receive, O Lord, my morning sacrifice which I now offer up to thee; I yield thee humble and hearty thanks that thou hast preserved me from the dangers of the night past, and brought me to the light of this day, and the comforts thereof, a day which is consecrated to thine own service and for thine honour. Let my heart, therefore, Gracious God, be so affected with the glory and majesty of it, that I may not do mine own works, but wait on thee, and discharge those weighty duties thou requirest of me; and since thou art a God of pure eyes, and wilt be sanctified in all who draw near unto thee, who doest not regard the sacrifice of fools, nor hear sinners who tread in thy courts, pardon, I beseech thee, my sins, remove them from thy presence, as far as the east is from the west, and accept of me for the merits of thy son Jesus Christ, that when I come into thy temple, and compass thine altar, my prayer may come before thee as incense; and as thou wouldst hear me calling upon thee in my prayers, so give me grace to hear thee calling on me in thy word, that it may be wisdom, righteousness, reconciliation & peace to the saving of my soul in the day of the Lord Jesus.

Grant that I may hear it with reverence, receive it with meekness, mingle it with faith, and that it may accomplish in me, Gracious God, the good work for which thou hast sent it. Bless my family, kindred, friends and country, be our God & guide this day and for ever for his sake, who lay down in the Grave and arose again for us, Jesus Christ Our Lord. Amen.

SUNDAY EVENING.

O MOST Glorious God, in Jesus Christ my merciful & loving father, I acknowledge and confess my guilt, in the weak and imperfect performance of the duties of this day. I have called on thee for pardon and forgiveness of sins, but so coldly & carelessly, that my prayers are become my sin and stand in need of pardon. I have heard thy holy word, but with such deadness of spirit that I have been an unprofitable and forgetful hearer, so that, O Lord, tho' I have done thy work, yet it hath been so negligently that I may rather expect a curse than blessing from thee. But, O God, who art rich in mercy and plenteous in redemption, mark not, I beseech thee, what I have done amiss; remember I am but dust, and remit my transgressions, negligences & ignorances, and cover them all with the absolute obedience of thy dear Son, that those sacrifices which I have offered may be accepted by thee, in and for the sacrifice Jesus Christ offered upon the cross for me; for his sake, ease me of the burden of my sins, and give me grace that by the call of the Gospel I may rise from the slumber of sin unto newness of life. Let me live according to those holy rules which thou hast this day prescribed in thy holy word; make me to know what is acceptable in thy sight, and therein to delight. open the eyes of my understanding, and help me thoroughly to examine myself concerning my knowledge, faith and repentance. increase my faith, and direct me to the true object Jesus Christ the way, the truth and the life, bless, O Lord, all the people of this land, from the highest to the lowest, particularly those whom thou hast appointed to rule over us in church & state. continue thy goodness to me this night. These weak petitions I humbly implore thee to hear accept and ans. for the sake of thy Dear Son Jesus Christ our Lord. Amen.

MONDAY MORNING.

O ETERNAL and everlasting God, I presume to present myself this morning before thy Divine majesty, beseeching thee to accept of my humble and hearty thanks, that it hath pleased thy great goodness to keep and preserve me the night past from all the dangers poor mortals are subject to, and hast given me sweet and pleasant sleep, whereby I find my body refreshed and comforted for performing the duties of this day, in which I beseech thee to defend me from all perils of body & soul. Direct my thoughts, words and work, wash away my sins in the immaculate blood of the Lamb, and purge my heart by the holy spirit, from the dross of my natural corruption, that I may with more freedom of mind and liberty of will serve thee, the ever living God, in righteousness and holiness this day, and all the days of my life. Increase my faith in the sweet promises of the gospel; give me repentance from dead works; pardon my wanderings, & direct my thoughts unto thyself, the God of my salvation; teach me how to live in thy fear, labour in thy service, and ever to run in the ways of thy commandments; make me always watchful over my heart, that neither the terrors of conscience, the loathing of holy duties, the love of sin, nor an unwillingness to depart this life, may cast me into a spiritual slumber, but daily frame me more & more into the likeness of thy son Jesus Christ, that living in thy fear, and dying in thy favour, I may in thy appointed time attain the resurrection of the just unto eternal life bless my family, friends & kindred unite us all in praising & glorifying thee in all our works begun, continued, and ended when we shall come to make our last account before thee blessed saviour, who hath taught us thus to pray our Father, &c.

MONDAY EVENING.

MOST Gracious Lord God, from whom proceedeth every good and perfect gift, I offer to thy divine majesty my unfeigned praise & thanksgiving for all thy mercies towards me. Thou mad'st me at first and hast ever since sustained the work of thy own hand; thou gav'st thy Son to die for me; and hast given me assurance of salvation, upon my repentance and sincerely endeavouring to conform my life to his holy precepts and example. Thou art pleased to lengthen out to me the time of repentance, and to move me to it by thy spirit and by thy word, by thy mercies, and by thy judgments: out of a deepness of thy mercies, and my own unworthiness, I do appear before at this time; I have sinned and done very wickedly, be merciful to me, O God, and pardon me for

Jesus Christ sake: instruct me in the particulars of my duty, and suffer me not to be tempted above what thou givest me strength to bear. Take care, I pray thee of my affairs and more and more direct me in thy truth, defend me from my enemies, especially my spiritual ones. Suffer me not to be drawn from thee, by the blandishments of the world, carnal desires, the cunning of the devil, or deceitfulness of sin. work in me thy good will and pleasure, and discharge my mind from all things that are displeasing to thee, of all ill will and discontent, wrath and bitterness, pride & vain conceit of myself, and render me charitable, pure, holy, patient and heavenly minded. be with me at the hour of death; dispose me for it, and deliver me from the slavish fear of it, and make me willing and fit to die whenever thou shalt call me hence. Bless our rulers in church and state. bless O Lord the whole race of mankind, and let the world be filled with the knowledge of Thee and thy son Jesus Christ. Pity the sick, the poor, the weak, the needy, the widows and fatherless, and all that mourn or are broken in heart, and be merciful to them according to their several necessities. bless my friends and grant me grace to forgive my enemies as heartily as I desire forgiveness of Thee my heavenly Father. I beseech thee to defend me this night from all evil, and do more for me than I can think or ask, for Jesus Christ sake, in whose most holy name & words, I continue to pray, Our Father, &c.

TUESDAY MORNING.

O LORD our God, most mighty and merciful father, I thine unworthy creature and servant, do once more approach thy presence. Though not worthy to appear before thee, because of my natural corruptions, and the many sins and transgressions which I have committed against thy divine majesty; yet I beseech thee, for the sake of him in whom thou art well pleased, the Lord Jesus Christ, to admit me to render thee deserved thanks and praises for thy manifold mercies extended toward me, for the quiet rest & repose of the past night, for food, raiment, health, peace, liberty and the hopes of a better life through the merit of thy dear son's bitter passion. and O kind father continue thy mercy and favour to me this day, and ever hereafter; prosper all my lawful undertakings; let me have all my directions from thy holy spirit, and success from thy bountiful hand. Let the bright beams of thy light so shine into my heart, and enlighten my mind in understanding thy blessed word, that I may be enable to perform thy will in all things, and effectually resist all temptations of the world, the flesh, and the devil. preserve and defend our rulers in church & state. bless the people of this land, be a father to the fatherless, a comforter to the comfortless, a deliverer to the captives, and a physician to the sick. let thy blessing be upon our friends, kindred and families. Be our guide this day and forever through J.C. in whose blessed form of prayer I conclude my weak petitions — Our Father, &c.

TUESDAY EVENING.

MOST gracious God and heavenly father, we cannot cease, but must cry unto thee for mercy, because my sins cry against me for justice. How shall I address myself unto thee, I must with the publican stand and admire at thy great goodness, tender mercy, and long suffering towards me, in that thou hast kept me the past day from being consumed and brought to nought. O Lord, what is man, or the son of man, that thou regardest him; the more days pass over my head, the more sins and iniquities I heap up against thee. If I should cast up the account of my good deeds done this day, how few and small would they be; but if I should reckon my miscarriages, surely they would be many and great. O, blessed Father, let thy son's blood wash me from all impurities, and cleanse me from the stains of sin that are upon me. Give me grace to lay hold upon his merits; that they may be my reconciliation and atonement unto thee, — That I may know my sins are forgiven by his death & passion. embrace me in the arms of thy mercy; vouchsafe to receive me into the bosom of thy love, shadow me with thy wings, that I may safely rest under thy protection this night; and so into thy hands I commend myself, both soul & body, in the name of thy son, J.C., beseeching Thee, when this life shall end, I may take my everlasting rest with thee in thy heavenly kingdom. bless all in authority over us, be merciful to all those afflicted with any cross or calamity. bless all my friends, forgive my enemies and accept of my thanksgiving this evening for all the mercies and favours afforded me; hear and graciously answer these my requests, and whatever else thou see'st needful grant us, for the sake of Jesus Christ in whose blessed name and words I continue to pray, Our Father, &c.

A PRAYER FOR WEDNESDAY MORNING.

ALMIGHTY and eternal Lord God, the great creator of heaven & earth, and the God and Father of our Lord Jesus Christ; look down from heaven, in pity and compassion upon me thy servant, who humbly prostrate myself before thee, sensible of thy mercy and my own misery; there is an infinite distance between thy glorious majesty and me, thy poor creature, the work of thy hand, between thy infinite power, and my weakness, thy wisdom, and my folly, thy eternal Being, and my mortal frame, but, O Lord, I have set myself at a greater distance from thee by my sin and wickedness, and humbly acknowledge the corruption of my nature and the many rebellions of my life. I have sinned against heaven and before thee, in thought, word & deed; I have contemned thy majesty and holy laws. I have likewise sinned by omitting what I ought to have done, and committing what I ought not. I have rebelled against light, despised thy mercies and judgments, and broken my vows and promises; I have neglected the means of Grace, and opportunities of becoming better; my iniquities are multiplied, and my sins are very great. I confess them, O Lord, with shame and sorrow, detestation and loathing, and desire to be vile in my own eyes, as I have rendered myself vile in thine. I humbly beseech thee to be merciful to me in the free pardon of my sins, for the sake of thy dear Son, my only saviour, J.C., who came not to call the righteous, but sinners to repentance; be pleased to renew my nature, and write thy laws upon my heart, and help me to live, righteously, soberly and godly in this evil world; make me humble, meek, patient, and contented, and work in me the grace of thy holy spirit. prepare me for death and judgment, and let the thoughts thereof awaken me to a greater care and study to approve myself unto thee in well doing. bless our rulers in church & state. Help all in affliction or adversity — give them patience and a sanctified use of their affliction, and in thy good time deliverance from them: forgive my enemies, take me into thy protection this day, keep me in perfect peace, which I ask in the name & for the sake of Jesus. Amen.

WEDNESDAY EVENING.

HOLY and eternal Lord God who art the King of heaven, and the watchman of Israel, that never slumberest or sleepest, what shall we render unto thee for all thy benefits: because thou hast inclined thine ear unto me, therefore will I call on thee as long as I live, from the rising of the sun to the going down of the same let thy name be praised. among the infinite riches of the mercy towards me, I desire to render thanks & praise for thy merciful preservation of me this day, as well as all the days of my life; and for the many other blessings & mercies spiritual & temporal which thou hast bestowed on me, contrary to my deserving[.] All these thy mercies call on me to be thankful and my infirmities & wants call for a continuance of thy tender mercies: cleanse my soul, O Lord, I beseech thee, from whatever is offensive to thee, and hurtful to me, and give me what is convenient for me. watch over me this night, and give me comfortable and sweet sleep to fit me for the service of the day following. Let my soul watch for the coming of the Lord Jesus; let my bed put me in mind of my grave, and my rising from there of my last resurrection; O heavenly Father, so frame this heart of mine, that I may ever delight to live according to thy will and command, in holiness and righteousness before thee all the days of my life. Let me remember, O Lord, the time will come when the trumpet shall sound, and the dead shall arise and stand before the judgment seat, and give an account of whatever they have done in the body, and let me so prepare my soul, that I may do it with joy and not with grief. bless the rulers and people of this and forget not those who are under any affliction or oppression. Let thy favour be extended to all my relations friends and all others who I ought to remember in my prayer and hear me I beseech thee for the sake of my dear redeemer in whose most holy words, I farther pray, Our Father, &c.

THURSDAY MORNING.

MOST gracious Lord God, whose dwelling is in the highest heavens, and yet beholdest the lowly and humble upon earth, I blush and am ashamed to lift up my eyes to thy dwelling place, because I have sinned against thee; look down, I beseech thee upon me thy unworthy servant who prostrate myself at the footstool of thy mercy, confessing my own guiltiness, and begging pardon for my sins; what couldst thou have done Lord more for me, or what could I have done more against thee? Thou didst send thy Son to take our nature upon

NOTE: The manuscript ended at this place, the close of a page. Whether the other pages were lost, or the prayers were never completed, has not been determined.

Index

Abbott, Lyman, 68–69
Abercrombie, James (doctor), 1–2
Alexandria (Virginia), 16, 62
Alexandria Parish (Virginia), 47
Armstrong, John, 71–72
Baltimore, 43
Baptists, 12, 31–33
Barry, John, 27
Bassett, Burwell, 5
Braddock, Edward (British general), 6, 62–63
Belvoir (Fairfax estate), 4
Benjamin, W. E., 64, 67
Boller, Paul F., 3 and saying of grace, 3–4
Burk, William Herbert, 52, 56–57

Charleston (South Carolina), 42
Chatterton Hill, 70
Christ Church (Alexandria), 17, 48
Christ Church (Philadelphia), 1
Civil War, 18-19
Comber, Thomas, 62
Connecticut, 3
Constitutional Convention, 8, 32

Continental army, 19, 21–23
Continental Congress, 10, 13, 23
Cornwallis, Lord, 8
Cross Roads (Virginia), 26
Custis, John Parke, 49
Custis, Nelly, 1; assessment of Washington's religious life, 47–50, 61
Custis, Patsy, 18, 49

"Daily Sacrifice," 51–116; illustrations, 83–106; transcription, 107–16
Dewees, William, 23–24
Dinwiddie, Robert (governor), 64
Dogue Run (farm), 16
Duportail (French general), 23

Ellezy, Tazewell, 27
Episcopal Church (Philadelphia), 45

Fairfax, Bryan, 62
Fairfax, George William, 27
Fairfax County (Virginia), 26, 47
Fairfax Parish (Virginia), 47

Federal City (District of Columbia), 47
Ford, Paul Leicester, 59
Fort Loudon, 70
Franklin, Benjamin, 4
Freemasonry, 4
French, Daniel, 16, 26–27
French and Indian War, 6, 9, 70–71

Gardner, William, 27
Gibson, —— (bishop), 59
Great Meadows, 62

Hewes, Caleb, 23
Hewes, Deborah Pyewell Potts, 23
Hoffman, Charles Frederick (reverend), 66, 68
Hollis, ——, 26
Howe, William (British general), 23

Jefferson, Thomas, 4
Jews, 10, 12, 28, 38–39, 41-43
Johnstone, William Jackson, 52

Kalb, Johann, 79

Lancaster (Pennsylvania), 23
Lewis, Betty Washington, 8
Lewis, Eleanor Parke Custis. *See* Custis, Nelly
Lewis, J. R. C., 51, 64
Lewis, Robert, 61–62

McCarty, Daniel, 27

Madison, James, 4, 10, 28
Mason, George, 15–16, 27, 28–29
Massey, Lee (reverend), 18
Meade, William (bishop), 60
Montgomery County (Pennsylvania), 23
Mount Vernon, 1, 9, 16, 28, 47, 49, 62
Muslims, 10, 28

Newburgh (New York), 13
Newport (Rhode Island), 41
New Church (Baltimore), 43
New England, 3
New York City, 29, 31, 33, 36, 42, 48

Payne, Edward, 27
Perkins, Isaac: tavern of, 3
Philadelphia, 1, 8, 23, 42, 45, 48
Philadelphia County (Pennsylvania), 23
Pohick Church, Truro Parish, 15–18; illustrations, 16, 17, 26–27, 47–48, 62
Pohick warehouse (Virginia), 26
Pond, Enoch, 1
Posey, John, 27
Potter, —— (doctor), 68
Potts, Isaac, 24; house of, 22–23; and Washington praying at Valley Forge, 19–20, 60, 70
Potts, John, 24
Potts, Sarah, 19–20, 24
Potts, Thomas II, 23
Presbyterians, 31, 33

Quakers, 12, 19–21, 23, 31, 34–35, 61, 70

Reformed German Congregation (New York City), 29–30
Richmond (Virginia), 42
Robinson, Lucien M., 68
Roman Catholics, 12, 31, 36–38
Rose Hill (Virginia estate), 16

St. Paul's Chapel (New York City), 1
St. Peter's Church (Philadelphia), 1
Savannah (Georgia), 38
Schuylkill River, 23
Snowden, Nathaniel Randolph (reverend), 24
Society of Friends. *See* Quakers
Sparks, Jared, 47, 61

Revolutionary War, 6–8, 9–10, 12–14, 18, 19–24, 29–30

Taverns, 3
Trinity Church (New York City), 1
Truro Parish (Virginia), 1, 15–18, 26–27

Unitarian Universalists, 31, 39–40
United States Congress, 10, 47
Upham, S. F., 68–69

Valley Creek (Pennsylvania), 23
Valley Forge (Pennsylvania), 19–24; illustration, 22

Virginia General Assembly, 10

Washington, Augustine, 62
Washington, Bushrod, 49, 51, 64, 67
Washington, George: his belief in afterlife, 8–9; his Barbados diary, 53–54; his Bible records, 64; and chaplains, 9; his childhood, 3–4; his church attendance, 47–48; his church pew, 18, 47–48; his circular letter to governors, 13–14; and civil authority, 9, 12–13, 32, 35, 37, 41–42, 45, 46, 64; and Constitutional Convention, 8, 32; his correspondence, 13, 25–47; and Deism, 4; his diaries, 1, 53–54, 60; and Episcopalian Church, 1, 26–27; his faith, 7; his family, 1–3, 5, 8–9, 18, 47–50; his Farewell Address, 10–11, 77–79; his Farewell Orders, 8; and Freemasonry, 4; and French and Indian War, 6, 9, 70–71; his general orders, 7–8; his handwriting, 51, 53–54, 67; his headquarters, 23; his library, 62–63; and Lord's Supper, 1–3, 48, 49; his marriage, 1; his mottos, 50; Nelly Custis's assessment of, 47–50, 61; his presidency, 1–2, 39, 48, 62, 76, 79; and Providence, 4–8, 12, 13, 35, 37, 44; and public support of religion,

10; ; and religious liberty, 9–10, 12, 30, 34, 35–36, 37, 40, 41, 42, 44; his religious terminology, 4–6, 8–9, 12, 14, 32, 34, 35, 38, 39, 43, 76; and Revolutionary War, 6–8, 9–10, 12–14, 18, 19–24, 30, 32, 34, 35–36; 37, 71–72; his Rules of Civility, 64; and saying of grace, 3; sets example, 2–3; his signature in books, 62; so-called prayer of, 14; so-called prayer book of, 51–116; and Stoicism, 4; as surveyor, 16; his travels, 7, 9; his praying at Valley Forge, 19-24; his vestry service, 1, 15–16, 18, 26–27; his vine and fig tree metaphor, 42

Washington, Lawrence, 64, 67

Washington, Jane C., 67

Washington, John Augustine, 67

Washington, Martha, 2, 48, 49–50, 70, 72

Washington, Mary, 8–9, 62–63

Washington, Thomas B., 51, 64

Washington Memorial Chapel (Valley Forge): illustration, 56, 79

Weems, Mason Locke: and Washington praying at Valley Forge, 19-24

White Plains (New York), 7

Wilson, Thomas (bishop), 62

The Ways of Providence: Religion and George Washington
is adapted from Frank E. Grizzard, Jr.'s
George! A Guide to All Things Washington
(Buena Vista and Charlottesville, Virginia, 2005)
and from
William Herbert Burk's *Washington's Prayers*
(Norristown, Pennsylvania, 1907).

Printed in the United States
83079LV00006B/217-264/A